THE GLUE METHOD
FOR DRUM SET SOLOING

by James Murphy

Executive producer: Rob Wallis

Edited by Joe Bergamini

Cover design: Terry Branam

Music engraving: James Murphy

Book layout: Terry Branam

VIDEO FILES: DOWNLOAD or STREAM

To access the video content that comes with this book, go to:
https://www.halleonard.com/mylibrary
Enter code: **6483-0833-5704-8910**

www.hudsonmusic.com

Table of Contents

I dedicate this book to my mom and dad for never giving up on finding what I was good at and for all the hours you let me smash my drums in your basement... they paid off.

Introduction

I wanted to gain freedom and flow while soloing; I wanted it bad. But, like many drummers, I struggled with the art of soloing and the ability to play a solo freely and musically without the constant burden of which idea to play next while staying in the moment. *The Glue Method for Drum Set Soloing* was born from my own struggles to solo and has given me the musical freedom to spontaneously connect ideas without hesitation at multiple note rates while soloing. If you've experienced similar frustrations, this book is for you! Keep reading!

So, what is the Glue Method? The Glue Method is my approach to spontaneously connect ideas quickly and effortlessly with Glue Stickings while soloing, to gain musical freedom, and to stay connected to the composition in the moment. So, what is a Glue Sticking? A Glue Sticking is a grouping of simple stickings that are used consecutively, interchangeably, and applied musically to bridge more complex ideas. Glue Stickings, unlike chops, are easy to play technically and can be developed easily. We will break down the three categories of Glue Stickings and the four steps of development to learn, apply, and mix and match Glue Stickings. The four steps of development are equally, if not more, important than the stickings themselves, because through the development process, you will gain different layers of muscle memory and organization. With muscle memory comes a control of the vocabulary and the ability to continuously play Glue Stickings effortlessly, while simultaneously being connected to the musical environment around you. This is where the magic happens, as you are truly able to listen to yourself musically and the musical environment. Glue Stickings are the building blocks to soloing freedom, as they are the *glue* that connect ideas quickly, allowing you to move freely from one idea to the next while expressing yourself musically in the moment. And, if you get stuck while soloing, Glue Stickings give you the ability to stay musical while refocusing your solo in real time.

In order to form this bond with the stickings, I will lay out the same steps and processes that I went through, not only to gain control of the stickings, but also organization of the stickings. The Glue Method is comprised of three categories of Glue Stickings: Single Kick Variations, Rudiment-Based Variations, and Consecutive Kick Variations. The four steps of development are: physical independence, audible independence, phrase breaking, and phrase mixing and matching. When practicing, the development of the Glue Method is very structured and mechanical. However, this structure transforms into spontaneous freedom behind the kit as you add more Glue Stickings to your bag. A selection of Glue Stickings, combined with muscle memory, creates the freedom to mix, match and connect ideas spontaneously into a seamless, musical flow while soloing. With this method, come and go freely in and out of the groove, or leave the groove, and create a solo based on an endless stream of ideas and Glue Stickings.

The Four Steps of Development

There are four steps of development that each category of Glue Stickings will be applied to. Each one of these steps was born out of a fundamental flaw in my playing. Once I worked with the step, that flaw was erased and replaced with a strong foundation on which to build the next step on. Having these steps in my practice routine kept me focused and relaxed, clear-headed and confident. Trust me, don't worry... just follow them... achieving freedom takes discipline in the practice room.

I
Physical Independence

In this step, we will use the note rates and Glue Stickings as a vehicle to master the first fundamental: physical independence. We will play the designated exercise as written against your left foot keeping 8th-note time. Through this exercise, you will gain physical confidence and control. In this step, you will simultaneously gain physical independence and a strong sense of the note rates. For me, overcoming this hurdle was the first step to feeling musical freedom during my solo.

II
Audible Independence

In this step, we will work on the ability to hear two things at once. I wanted the ability to hear the larger phrase that I was creating with my Glue Sticking choices, while also taking the music into consideration. We will train your ear to hear a specific cycle of Glue Stickings while paying attention to the metronome. There will be no physical timekeeping in this step. You will play each exercise in a specific sequence, orchestration, and dynamic against a metronome.

III
Phrase Breaking

I got tired of always being so concerned about what sticking or grouping could fit in a space. Getting to a musical hit or a cadence to a new section of a song, required anticipating what combination of stickings would fit in the space. In this step, we will work on phrasing with each category of Glue Stickings, as well as how to break the Glue Stickings to get where you need to go.

IV
Phrase Mixing and Matching

In this final step, we will mix and match Glue Stickings to create musical phrases that can be manipulated to get to cadences to a new section of a song or to a musical hit, while staying connected to your composition. This is the first time in the steps of development where all of the stickings meet each other using the fundamentals: note rate, orchestration, dynamics, and phrasing. We will be using 4- or 8-bar phrasing for this step.

Drum Key

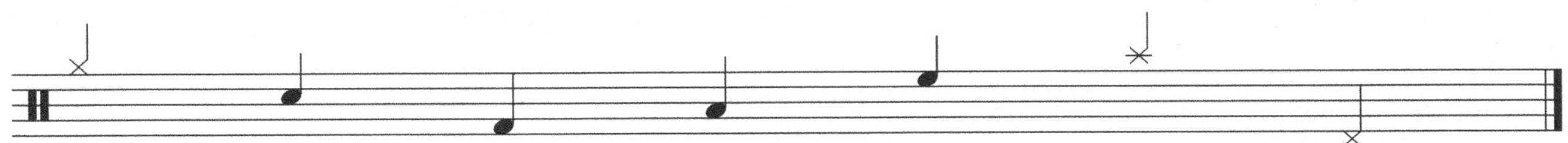

Sectioning Concept Diagram

Sectioning is an organizational concept that I developed to help with the application of specific categories of Glue Stickings to the drum set. Each category of stickings corresponds with a specific section of the drum set. The act of creating these sections, that pair with specific categories of Glue Stickings, gave me a deeper control of my organization, therefore freeing up more consciousness to be in the moment and explore the musicality of what I was playing.

I created the concept of sectioning to avoid the feeling of being overwhelmed by making choices during soloing. While soloing, a player has to make many musical choices including dynamics, rate change, and orchestration. The act of sectioning eliminates one choice, therefore creating more headspace to focus on dynamics and rate change, leading to more freedom and focus while soloing.

In Chapter 5, I will identify which category of Glue Stickings corresponds with each section of the drum set.

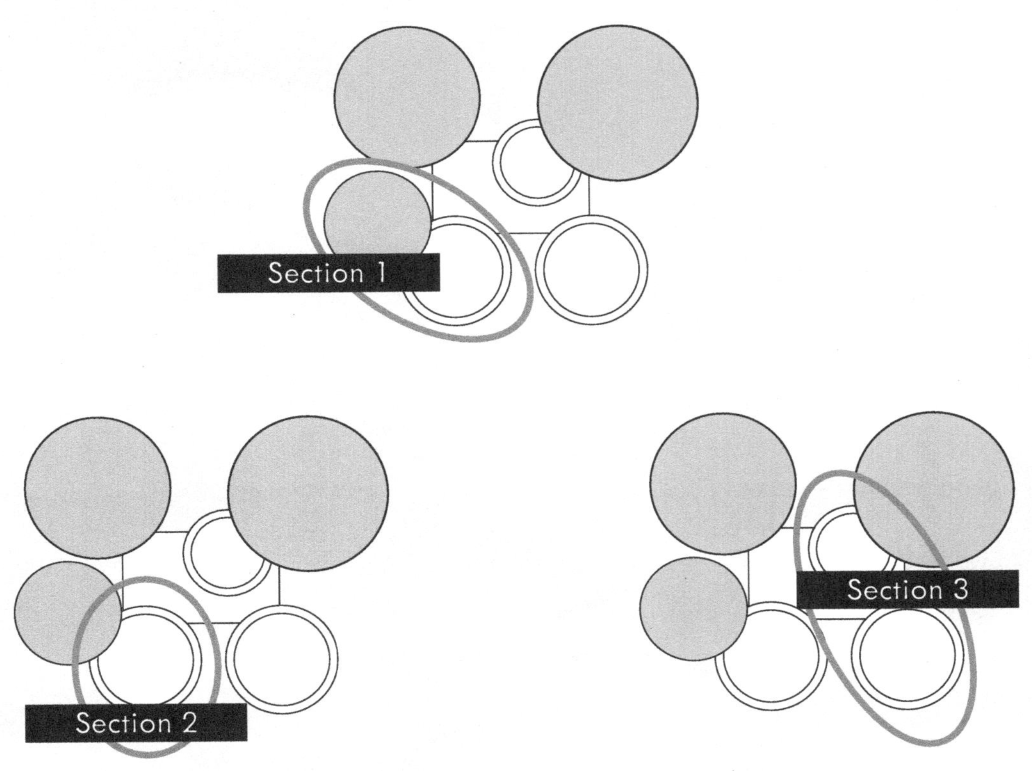

Star Description

Visualizing the Glue Method

This diagram is a visual representation of my organization and interpretation of where YOU fit into the Glue Method. "The Solo" is what drives us to find a method that will help identify a process that will guide us to get better at soloing. That is why I surrounded "The Solo" with the four steps of development: physical independence, audible independence, phrase breaking, and phrase mixing and matching. These steps had a positive impact on each fundamental that needed development in my playing. By developing each fundamental in this order, I was able to create a strong foundation which supported the most important component: "You." The reason I placed "You" at the top of the star is because that is what makes the Glue Method come alive. Bringing your own interpretation to dynamics, rate change, and orchestration in step 4, phrase mixing and matching, is what makes these stickings a vehicle for your musical choices. "You" represents your sound, your touch, and your musicality.

Star Diagram

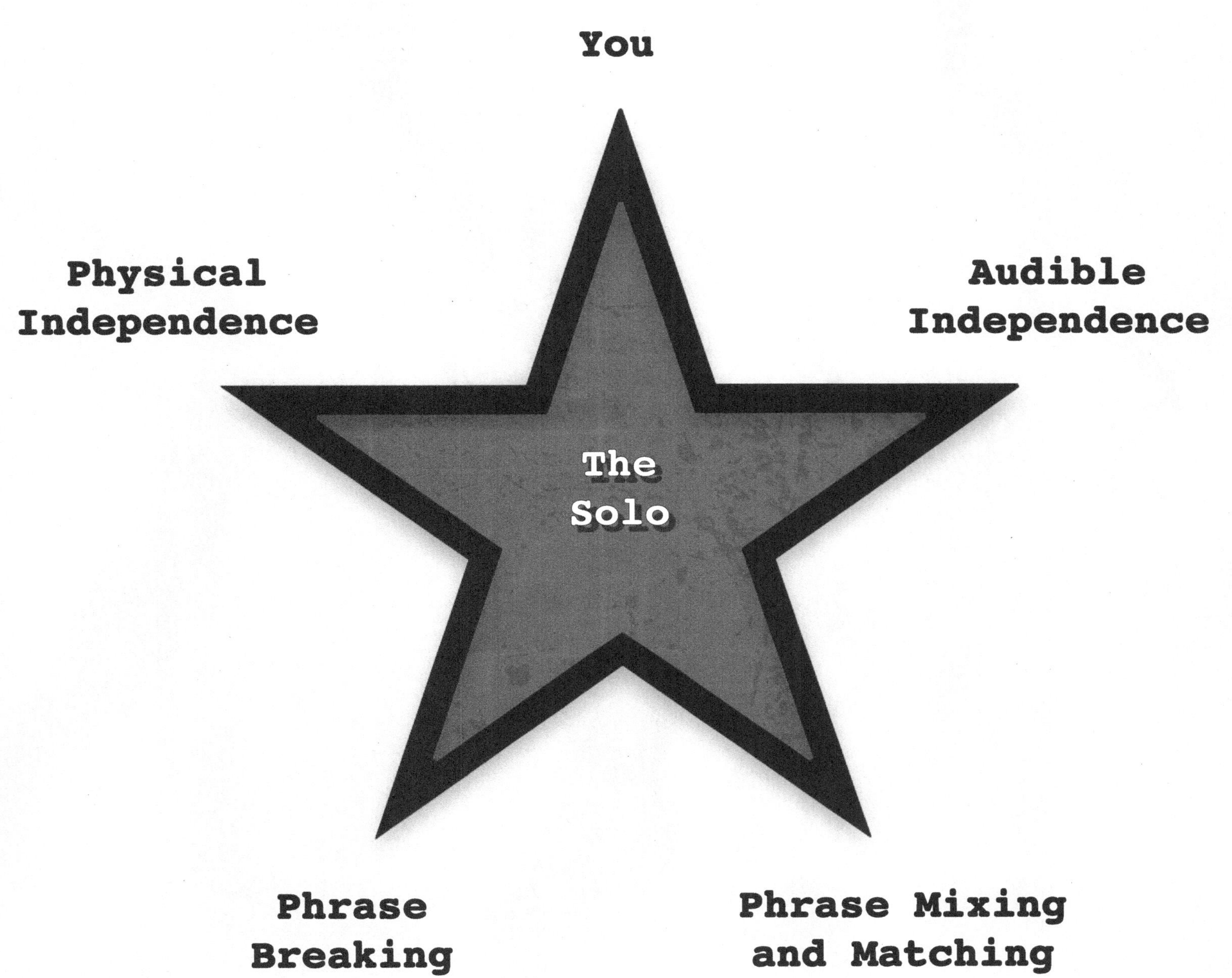

My dream for you...

...is to find your voice in the sea of stickings and for you to be able to create a musical solo while staying connected to your internal composition or with your live band, then getting off stage and feeling happy and proud of what you just created. That's the dream. *The Glue Method for Drum Set Soloing* made this dream a reality for me. This method gave me direction, organization, and freedom to something that used to make me feel lost and disorganized. This method was born out of my own struggles and self-doubt and developed into a world of freedom and creativity while soloing. Follow the method to find your touch; stickings are stickings, but the process in which we practice those stickings makes them our own.

CHAPTER 1
Single Kick Variations

Chapter 1

Glue Sticking Category #1

Single Kick Variations

This category of Glue Stickings has the description "Single Kick Variations" because of the implementation of only one kick per Glue Sticking. When I first started developing my vocabulary, I felt disorganized and overwhelmed with stickings. Creating smaller categories of stickings helped me to feel more empowered and focused, so that I could get through the designated stickings. Remember, organization can help to declutter your choices, therefore helping you to make better ones.

Chapter 1 Stickings Introduced

Single Kick Variations

RLLF

RLRLLF

RLRLRLLF

RRLLF

Chapter 1

Step I of Development

Physical Independence

In this step, we will use the note rates and Glue Stickings as a vehicle to master the first fundamental, physical independence. We will play the designated exercise as written against your left foot keeping 8th-note time. Through this exercise, you will gain physical confidence and control. In this step, you will simultaneously gain physical independence and a strong sense of the note rates. For me, overcoming this hurdle was the first step to feeling musical freedom during my solo.

Single Kick Variations

1st Glue Sticking: *RLLF*

Step 1: Perform 1st Glue Sticking at each designated note rate. Left foot keeps 8th note pulse with hi-hat. Also, apply these dynamic values one at a time. Metronome set at 50bpm.

Note Rate: 8th-Note Triplets (First Dynamic Shape)

Note Rate: 16th Notes

Note Rate: 16th-Note Triplets

Note Rate: 32nd Notes

Single Kick Variations

2nd Glue Sticking: *RLRLLF*

Step 1: Perform 2nd Glue Sticking at each designated note rate. Left foot keeps 8th-note pulse with hi-hat. Also, apply these dynamic values one at a time. Metronome set at 50bpm.

Dynamic Values

Note Rate: 8th-Note Triplets (First Dynamic Shape)

Note Rate: 16th Notes

Note Rate: 16th-Note Triplets

Note Rate: 32nd Notes

Single Kick Variations

3rd Glue Sticking: *RLRLRLLF*

Step 1: Perform 3rd Glue Sticking at each designated note rate. Left foot keeps 8th note pulse with hi-hat. Also, apply these dynamic values one at a time. Metronome set at 50bpm.

Dynamic Values

RLRLRLLF / RLRLRLLF / RLRLRLLF

Note Rate: 8th-Note Triplets (First Dynamic Shape)

Note Rate: 16th Notes

Note Rate: 16th-Note Triplets

Note Rate: 32nd Notes

Single Kick Variations

4th Glue Sticking: *RRLLF*

Step 1: Perform 4th Glue Sticking at each designated note rate. Left foot keeps 8th note pulse with hi-hat. Also, apply these dynamic values one at a time. Metronome set at 50bpm.

Dynamic Values

Note Rate: 8th-Note Triplets (First Dynamic Shape)

Note Rate: 16th Notes

Note Rate: 16th-Note Triplets

Note Rate: 32nd Notes

16

RRLLFRRLLFRRLLFRRLLFRRLLFRRLLFRR LLFRRLLFRRLLFRRLLFRRLLFRRLLFRRLL

Step II of Development

Audible Independence

In this step, we will work on the ability to hear two things at once. I wanted the ability to hear the larger phrase that I was creating with my Glue Sticking choices, while also taking into consideration the music. We will train your ear to hear a specific cycle of Glue Stickings while paying attention to the metronome. There will be no physical timekeeping in this step. You will play each exercise in a specific sequence, orchestration, and dynamic against a metronome.

Single Kick Variations

Creating Cycles

Step 2: Perform each of the "Single Kick Variation" stickings in three voice orchestration (kick, snare, hi-hat) in the order you find below. You will play through each sticking two times without stopping in between each sticking. This creates the cycle. Also, you will be using a new set of dynamic values. Metronome set at 50bpm.

Dynamic Values

RLLF / RLRLLF / RLRLRLLF / RRLLF

Cycle Applied to 8th-Note Triplets

Cycle Applied to 16th Notes

18

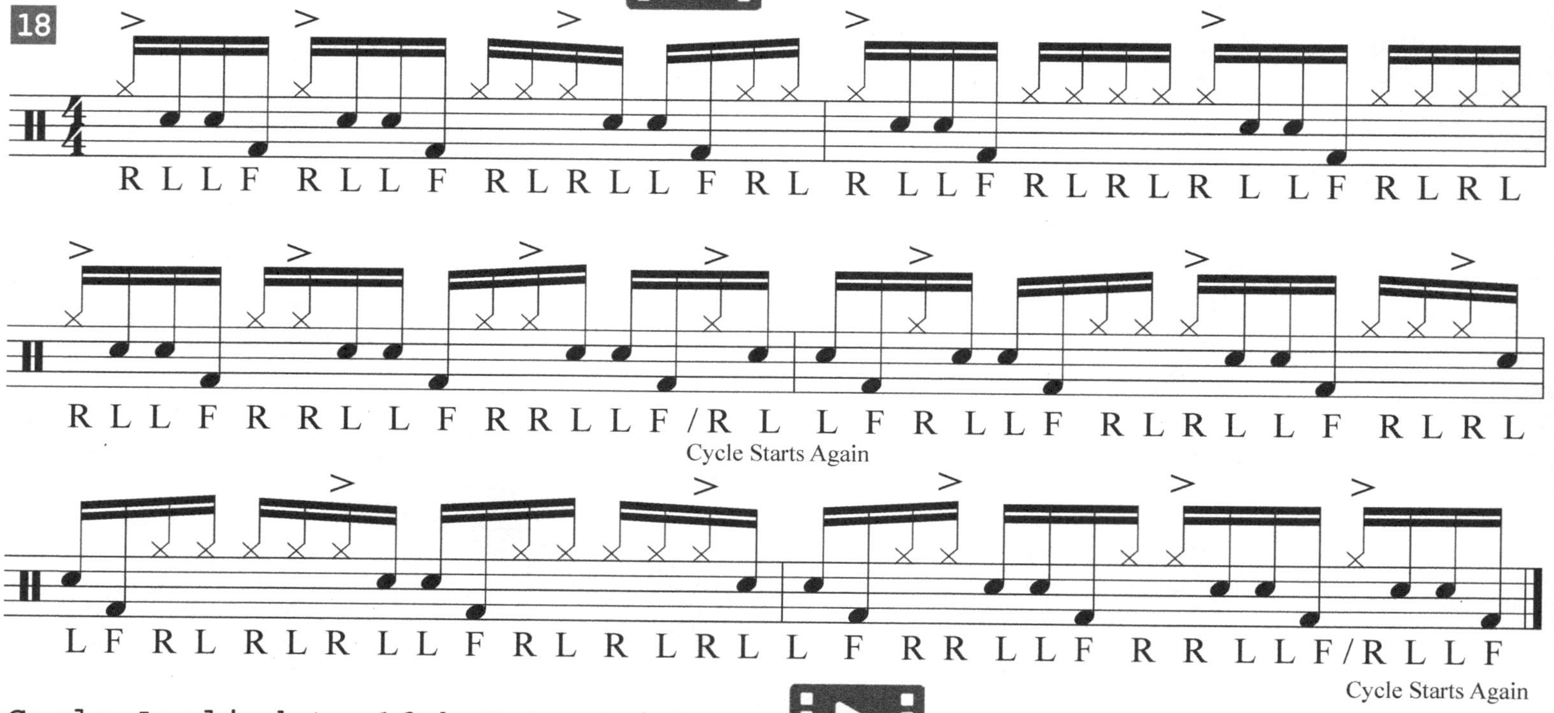

R L L F R L L F R L R L L F R L R L L F R L R L R L L F R L R L
R L L F R R L L F R R L L F / R L L F R L L F R L R L L F R L R L
Cycle Starts Again
L F R L R L R L L F R L R L R L L F R R L L F R R L L F / R L L F
Cycle Starts Again

Cycle Applied to 16th-Note Triplets

19

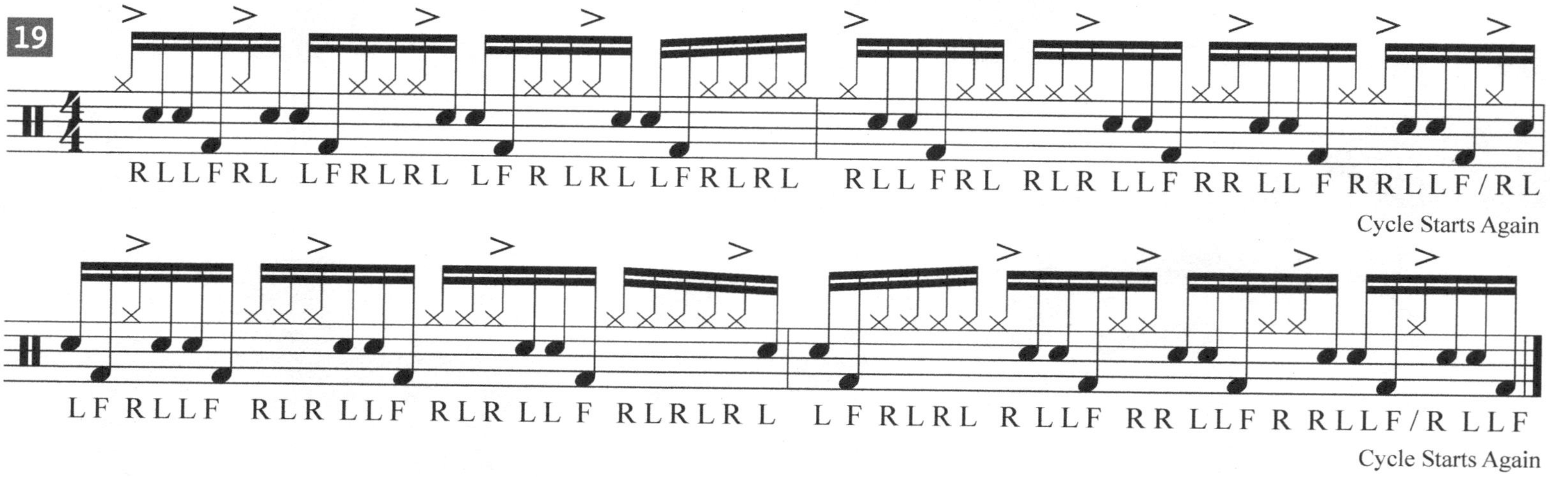

R L L F R L L F R L R L L F R L R L L F R L R L R L L F R L R L R L L F R R L L F R R L L F / R L
Cycle Starts Again
L F R L L F R L R L L F R L R L L F R L R L R L L F R L R L R L L F R R L L F R R L L F / R L L F
Cycle Starts Again

Cycle Applied to 32nd Notes

20

Cycle Starts Again
R L L F R L L F R L R L L F R L R L L F R L R L R L L F R L R L R L L F R R L L F R R L L F / R L L F R L L F R L R L L F R L R L
L F R L R L R L L F R L R L R L L F R R L L F R R L L F / R L L F
Cycle Starts Again

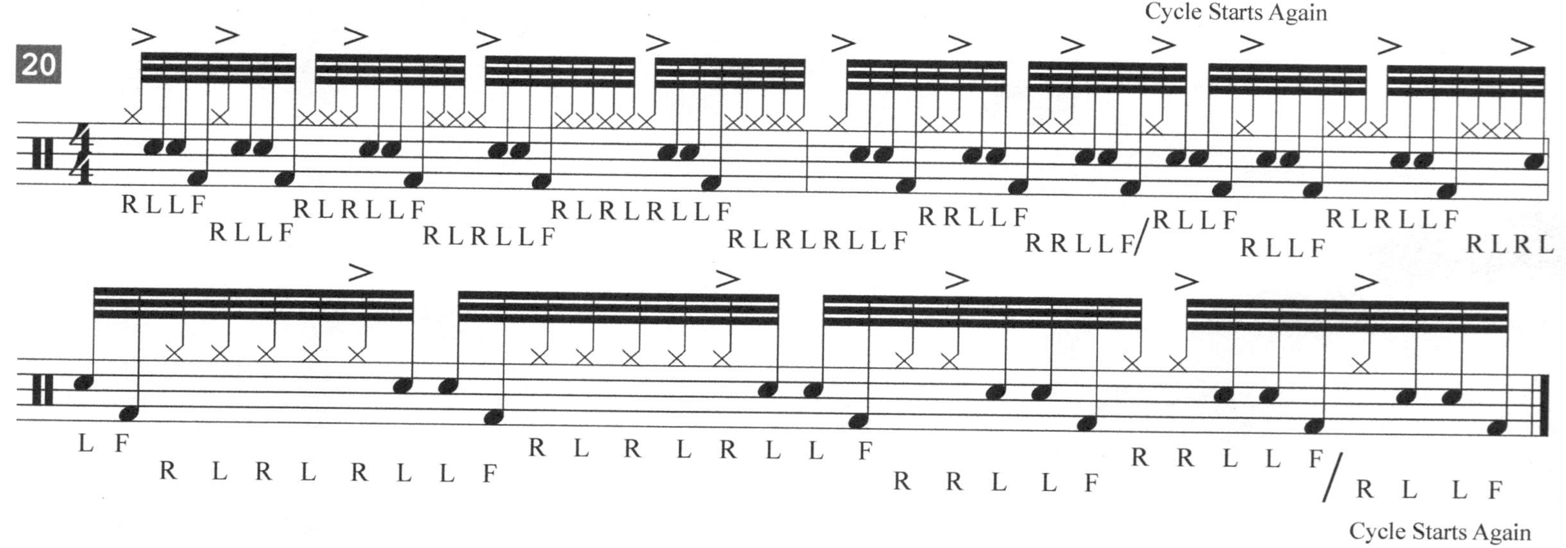

Step III of Development 

Phrase Breaking

I got tired of always being so concerned about what sticking or grouping could fit in a space. Getting to a musical hit or a cadence to a new section of a song required anticipating what combination of stickings would fit in the space. In this step, we will work on phrasing with each category of Glue Stickings, as well as how to break the Glue Stickings to get where you need to go.

Single Kick Variations

Glue Stickings Included

-RLLF-
-RLRLLF-
-RLRLRLLF-
-RRLLF-

Step 3: You will choose one Glue Sticking at a time, performed consecutively, applied to one chosen note rate. Continue to make choices with an improvisational function utilizing a 4-bar phrase format. At the end of the 4th bar, you will crash on the 1 with the idea that you are allowed to break any of the chosen Glue Stickings on the 4th beat of the 4th bar to get to the 1. This strengthened my ability to break my stickings to get to ensemble figures or natural cadences. As for the dynamic and orchestration choices, the only rule I followed was to keep it simple. If you have done your work with step 1 and 2, your body will make choices dynamically and musically from those steps. Left foot will be involved with holding the hi-hat in the down position. Metronome set at 50bpm.

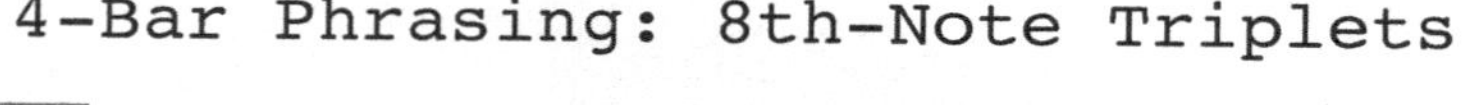

4-Bar Phrasing: 8th-Note Triplets

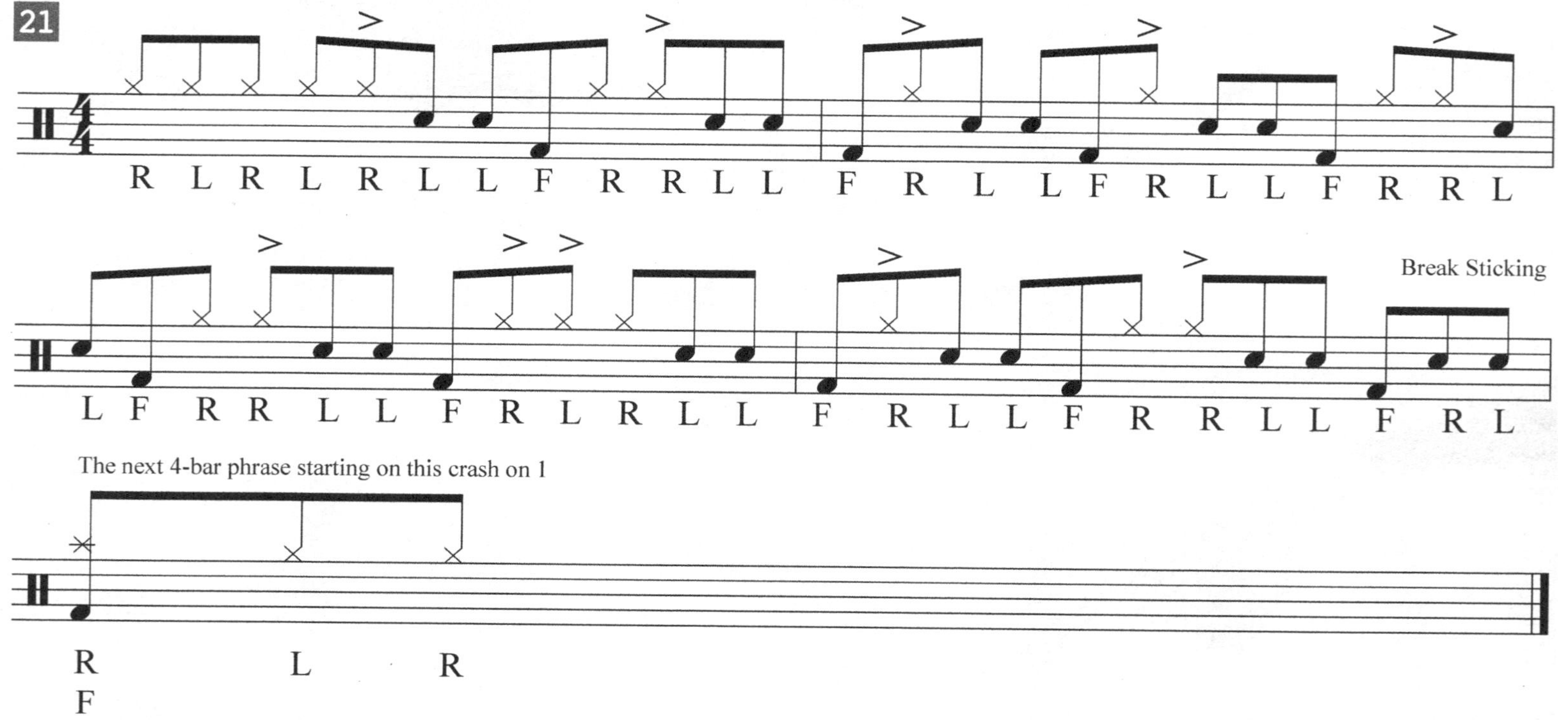

4-Bar Phrasing: 16th Notes

4-Bar Phrasing: 16th-Note Triplets

4-Bar Phrasing: 32nd Notes

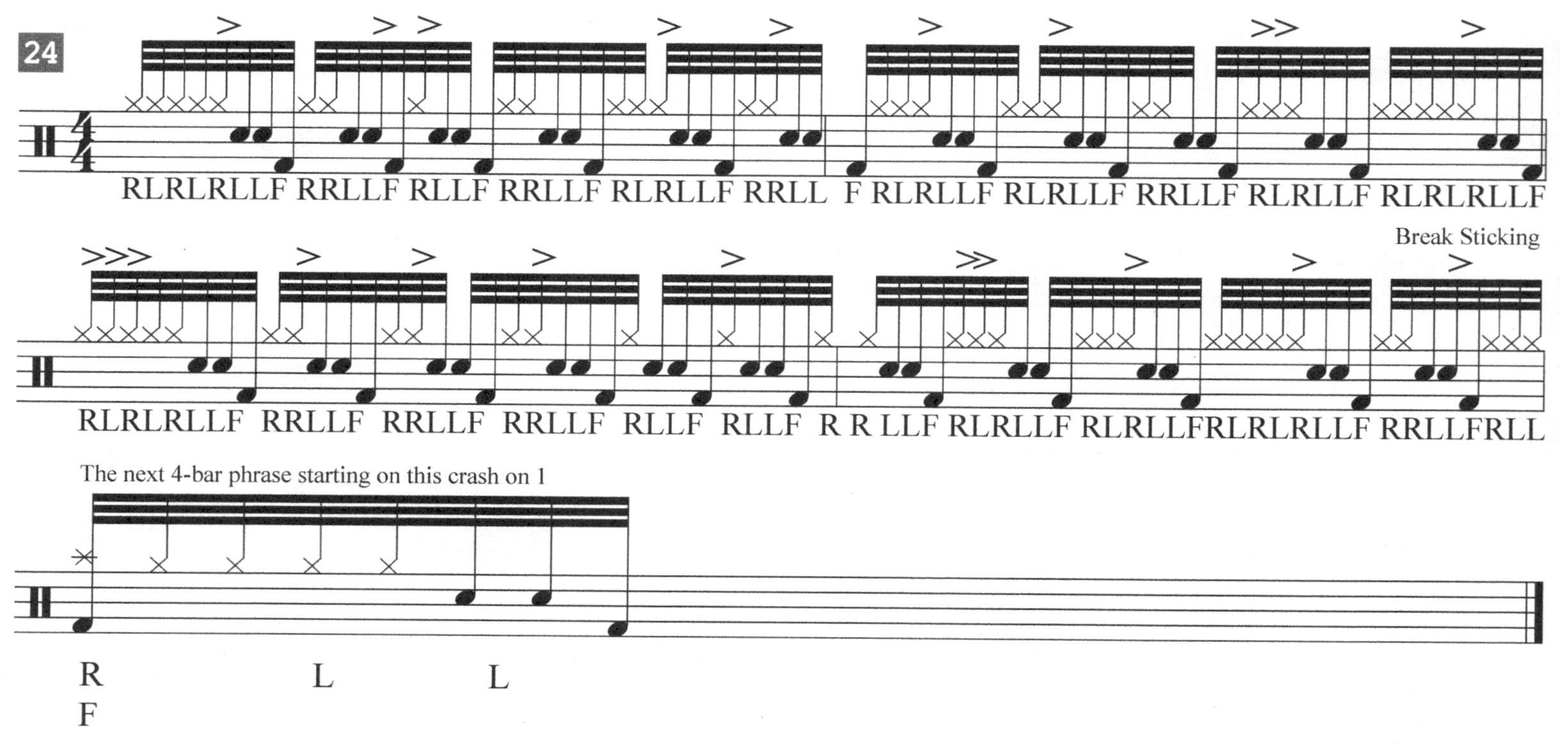

Chapter 1

Step IV of Development 

Phrase Mixing and Matching

In this final step, we will mix and match Glue Stickings to create musical phrases that can be manipulated to get to cadences to a new section of a song or a musical hit, while staying connected to your composition. This is the first time in the steps of development where all of the stickings meet each other using the fundamentals: note rate, orchestration, dynamics, and phrasing. We will be using 4- or 8-bar phrasing for this step.

Glue Stickings Included

-RLLF-

-RLRLLF-

-RLRLRLLF-

-RRLLF-

Step 4: You will choose one Glue Sticking at a time, performed consecutively, applied to all note rates introduced thus far. You will again use improvisation to choose your Glue Stickings while utilizing a 4-bar phrase format. At the end of the 4th bar, you will crash on the 1, with the idea that you are allowed to break any of the chosen Glue Stickings on the 4th beat of the 4th bar to get to the 1. We are continuing to strengthen the ability to break stickings, while adding a stronger element of musicality. Remember, continuing to loop the 4-bar phrase after you crash on the 1 is important… "DON'T STOP"; that's what I yell at my students. Left foot keeps 8th note pulse with hi-hat if you are not utilizing your hi-hat in a closed state. Metronome set at 50bpm.

4-Bar Phrasing: All note rates included with minimal orchestration

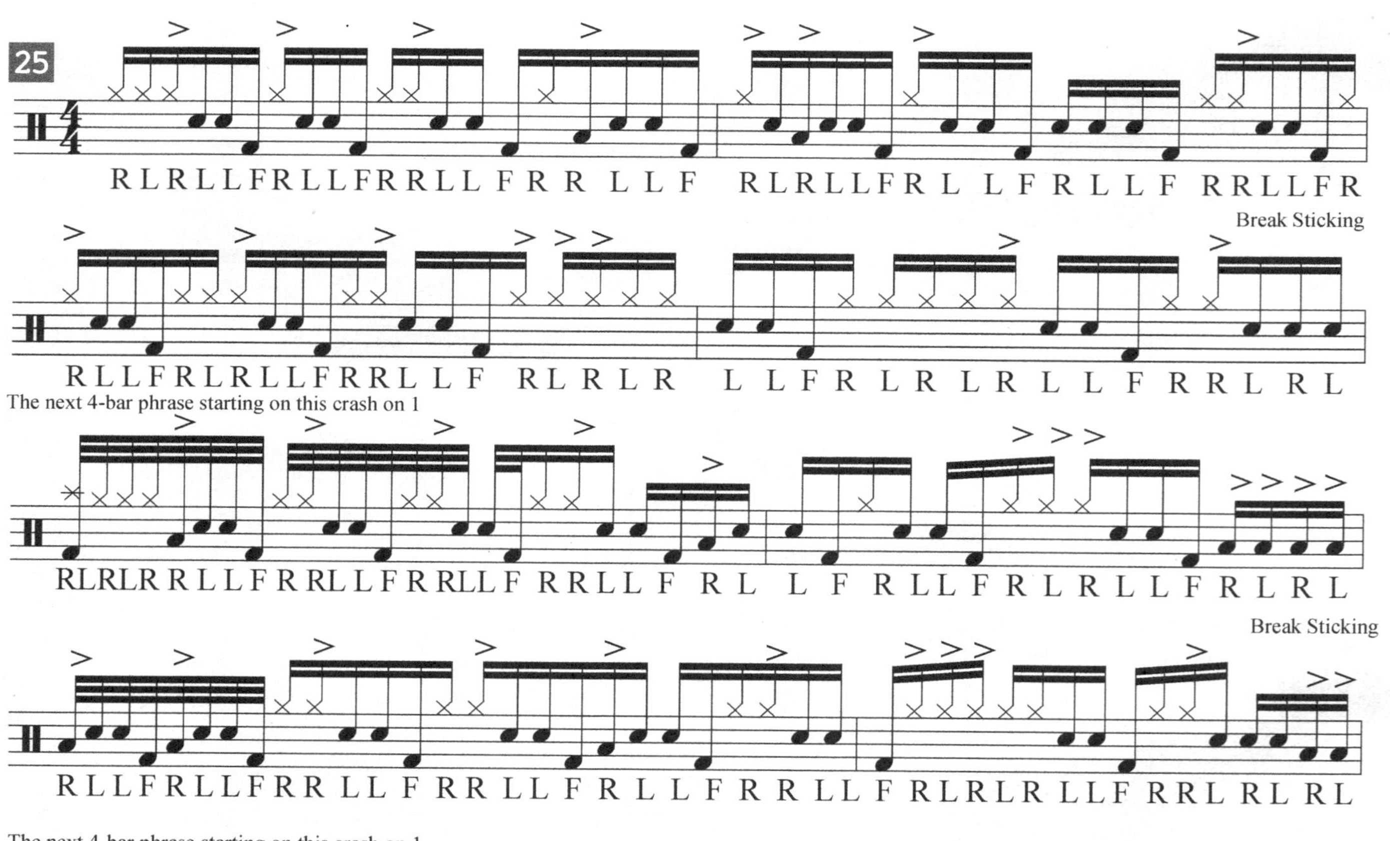

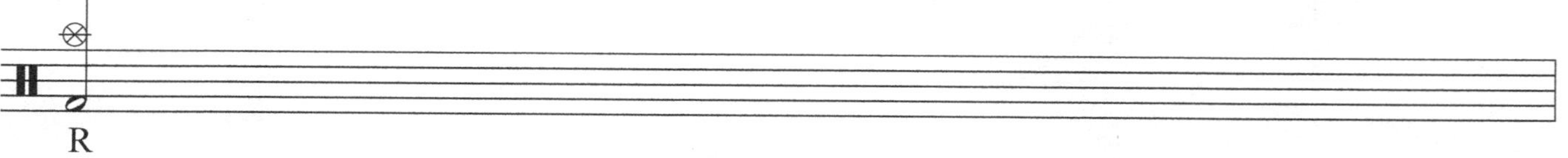

CHAPTER 2
Rudiment-Based Variations

Chapter 2

Glue Sticking Category #2

Rudiment-Based Variations

Being creative with what you already have is important, but taking what you already have and applying it to a set method of practicing is also important. "Rudiment-Based Variations" is made of a group of stickings that I had already had a grasp on.

Chapter 2 Stickings Introduced

Rudiment-Based Variations

RLLRRL

RLLR

RLLRRLRRLL

RLLRRLL

Chapter 2

Step I of Development

Physical Independence

Step 1 will still represent the development of physical independence, but you will notice that each new set of Glue Stickings will present a different challenge based on the limbs that are included in the specific stickings. Be aware of your body and how it is responding to the change in balance and physical demands per the new stickings in this chapter. This step is not about musicality, rather a focus on the body. Be patient and make sure to lengthen the amount of time you spend playing each sticking. The Glue Stickings in this chapter are physically easier to perform. Continue to evaluate your body's balance while the right leg is at rest.

1st Glue Sticking: *RLLRRL*

Step 1: Perform 1st Glue Sticking at each designated note rate. Left foot keeps 8th note pulse with hi-hat. Also, apply these dynamic values one at a time. Metronome set at 50bpm.

Dynamic Values

>RLLRRL> / >RLLRRL / RLLRRL>

Note Rate: 8th-Note Triplets (First Dynamic Shape)

26

Note Rate: 16th Notes

27

Note Rate: 16th-Note Triplets

28

Note Rate: 32nd Notes

29

2nd Glue Sticking: *RLLR*

Step 1: Perform 2nd Glue Sticking at each designated note rate. Left foot keeps 8th note pulse with hi-hat. Also, apply these dynamic values one at a time. Metronome set at 50bpm.

Dynamic Values

>
RLLR / RLLR

Note Rate: 8th-Note Triplets (First Dynamic Shape)

Note Rate: 16th Notes

Note Rate: 16th-Note Triplets

Note Rate: 32nd Notes

3rd Glue Sticking: *RLLRR LRRLL*

Step 1: Perform 3rd Glue Sticking at each designated note rate. Left foot keeps 8th note pulse with hi-hat. Also, apply these dynamic values one at a time. Metronome set at 50bpm.

Dynamic Values

> RLLRRLRRLL (accents over 1st and 6th notes) / **> RLLRRLRRLL** (accent over 1st note)

Note Rate: 8th-Note Triplets (First Dynamic Shape)

Note Rate: 16th Notes

Note Rate: 16th-Note Triplets

Note Rate: 32nd Notes

Rudiment-Based Variations

4th Glue Sticking: *RLLRRLL*

Step 1: Perform 4th Glue Sticking at each designated note rate. Left foot keeps 8th note pulse with hi-hat. Also, apply these dynamic values one at a time. Metronome set at 50bpm.

Dynamic Values

RLLRRLL / RLLRRLL

(accents: > on the first R of the first pattern; >> on the last two letters of the second pattern)

Note Rate: 8th-Note Triplets (First Dynamic Shape)

Note Rate: 16th Notes

Note Rate: 16th-Note Triplets

Note Rate: 32nd Notes

Chapter 2

Step II of Development

Audible Independence

In this step, you are relying on the physical independence that you developed in Step 1. With this independence, you are now able to listen to the musical shape of the stickings. The cycle, orchestrations, and dynamic values are the focus for this step. Step 2 is designed to get you to listen to the larger phrase (cycle) being created, rather than micromanaging the individual Glue Stickings. Honor the process; don't stray from the exercise or get distracted by trying to make these Glue Stickings creative at this point in the process. Creativity will come with time, as you gain the freedom developed through honoring the steps of development.

Creating Cycles

Step 2: Perform each of the "Rudiment-Based Variation" stickings in two voice orchestration (snare, hi-hat) in the order you find below. You will play through each sticking two times without stopping in between each sticking. This creates the cycle. Also, you will be using a new set of dynamic values.
Metronome set at 50bpm.

Dynamic Values

RLLRRL / RLLR / RLLRRLRRLL / RLLRRLL

Cycle Applied to 8th-Note Triplets

Cycle Applied to 16th Notes

43

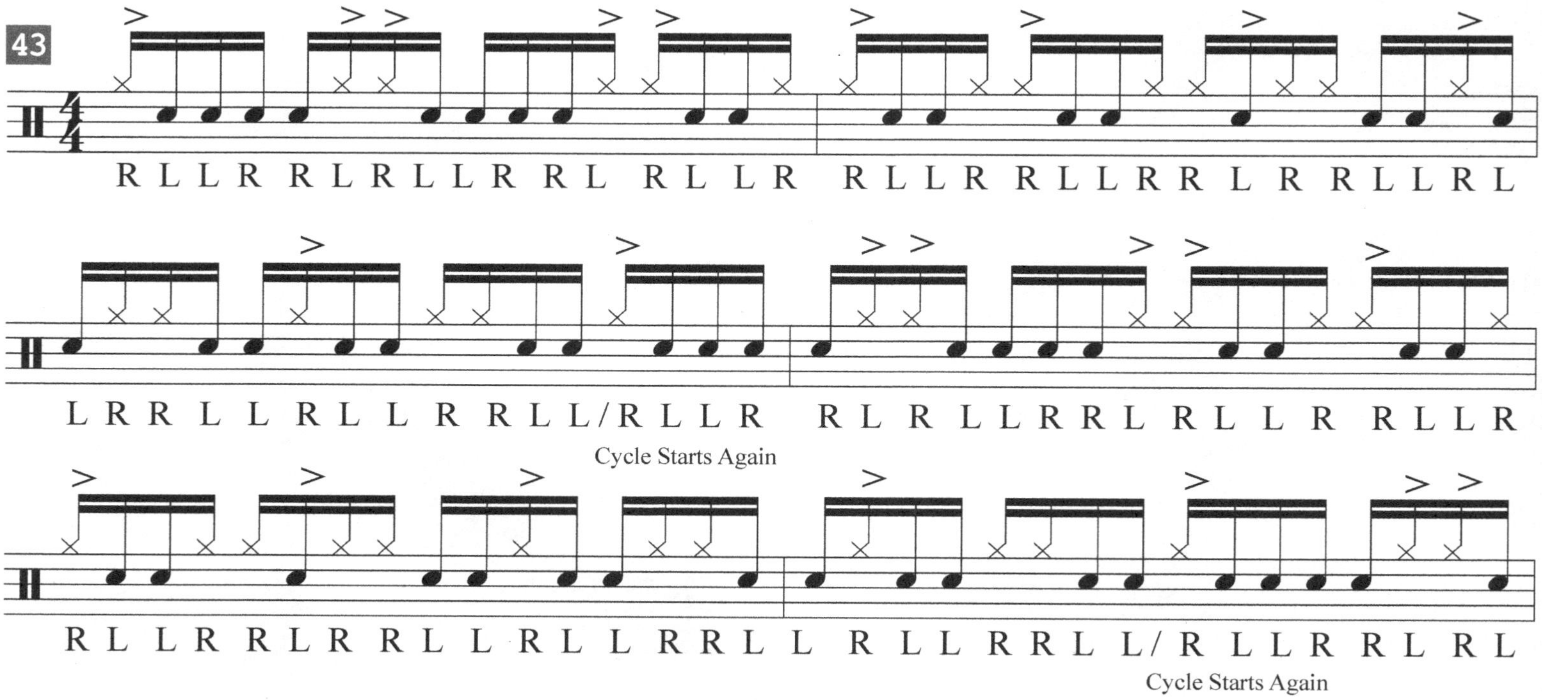

R L L R R L R L L R R L R L L R R L L R R L L R R L R R L L R L
L R R L L R L L R R L L/R L L R R L R L L R R L R L L R R L L R
Cycle Starts Again
R L L R R L R R L L R L L R R L L R L L R R L L/ R L L R R L R L
Cycle Starts Again

Cycle Applied to 16th-Note Triplets

44

RLLRRL RLLRRL RL LRRLLRR L LR RL RRLL RLL RRL LRLL R RLL/RLLR
Cycle Starts Again
RLRLLR R LRLL R RLL RR L LRRL RR L LRLLR R LLR LL RR LL/R LLRR LRL
Cycle Starts Again

Cycle Applied to 32nd Notes

45

RLLRRLRLLRRLRLLRRLLRRLLRRLRRLLRL LRRLLRLLRRLL/RLLRRLRLLRRLRLLRRLLR
Cycle Starts Again
R L L R R L R R L L R L L R R L L R L L R R L L /R L L R R L R L
Cycle Starts Again

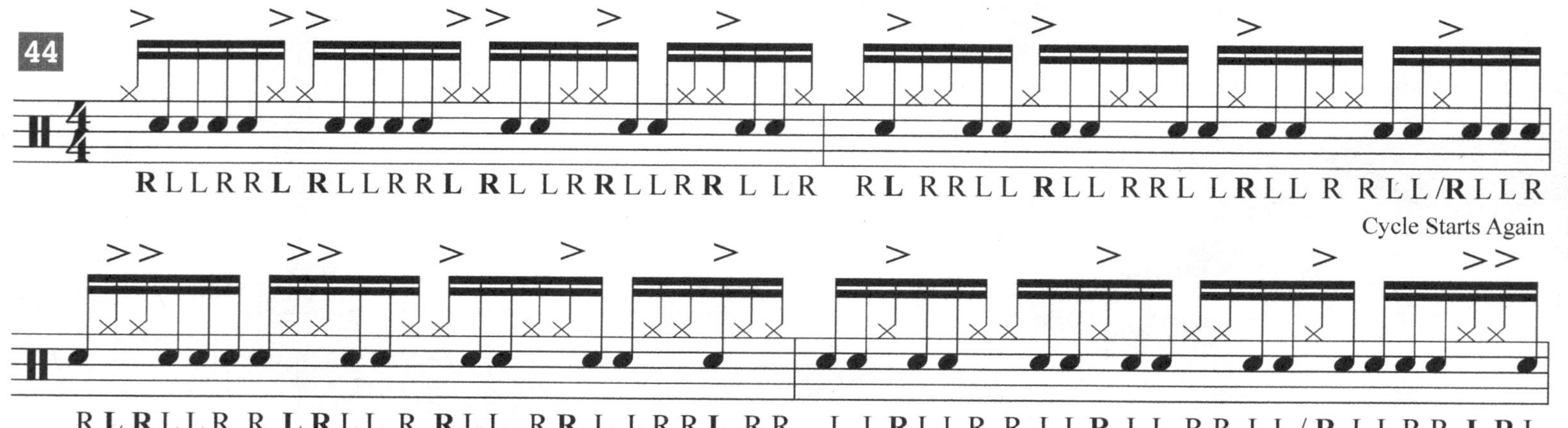

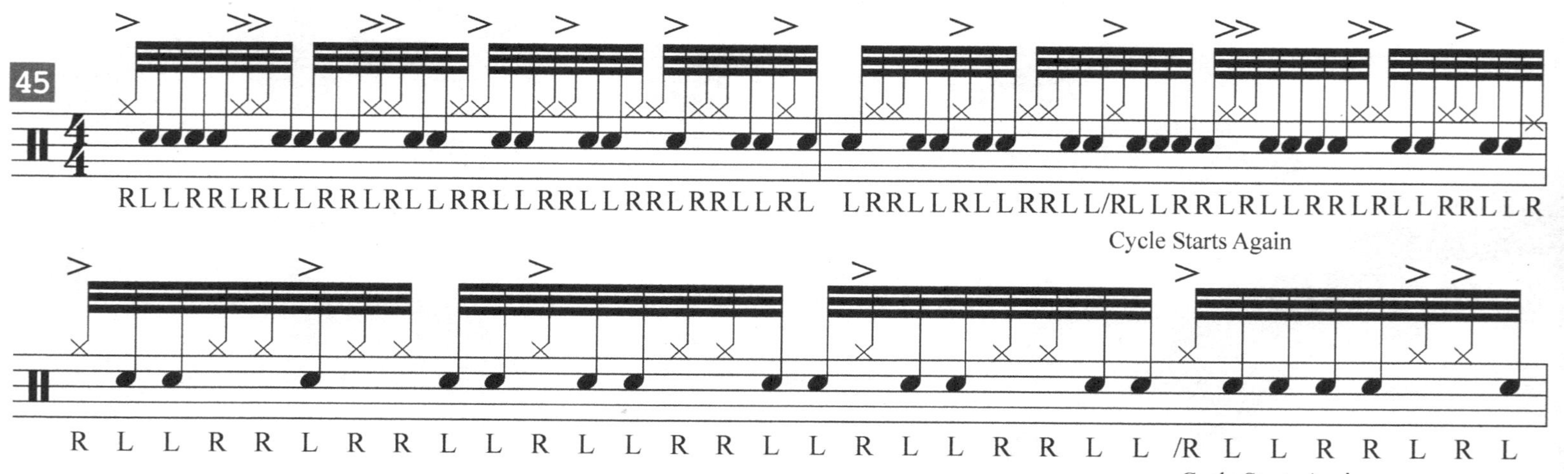

Chapter 2

Step III of Development

Phrase Breaking

The goal of phrase breaking is to develop the skill to break a Glue Sticking as close to the 1 as possible and then to improvise to get to the 1. When phrase breaking, try to get the Glue Stickings as close to the 1 as possible before breaking the phrase. Doing this, allows you to develop the ability to manipulate the Glue Stickings to get to musical hits or cadences. When improvising, keep your choices simple and don't try to put too much in when breaking the phrase. Remember, the phrase is defined by the amount of bars you will be improvising with using the Glue Stickings in this chapter. Having the ability to connect what you are playing to the musical application is the goal. Your body needs to understand where and how to leave the Glue Stickings if needed to make that connection.

Glue Stickings Included

-RLLRRL-
-RLLR-
-RLLRRLRRLL-
-RLLRRLL-

Step 3: You will choose one Glue Sticking at a time, performed consecutively, applied to one chosen note rate. Continue to make choices with an improvisational function utilizing a 4-bar phrase format. At the end of the 4th bar, you will crash on the 1 with the idea that you are allowed to break any of the chosen Glue Stickings on the 4th beat of the 4th bar to get to the 1. This strengthened my ability to break my stickings to get to ensemble figures or natural cadences. As for the dynamic and orchestration choices, the only rule I followed was to keep it simple. If you have done your work with step 1 and 2, your body will make choices dynamically and musically from those steps. The left foot will be involved with holding the hi-hat in the down position. Metronome set at 50bpm.

4-Bar Phrasing: 8th-Note Triplets

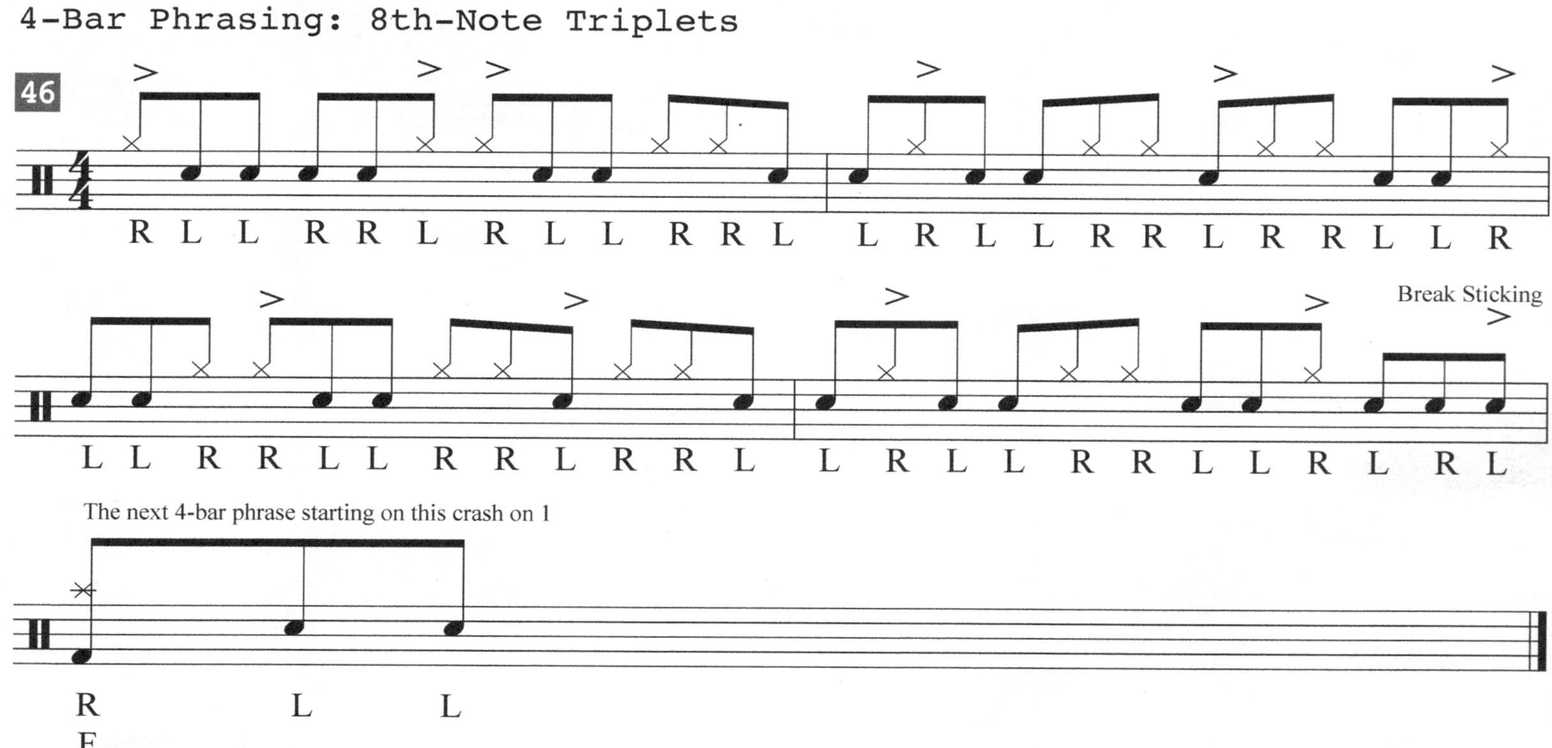

4-Bar Phrasing: 16th Notes

47

4-Bar Phrasing: 16th-Note Triplets

48

4-Bar Phrasing: 32nd Notes

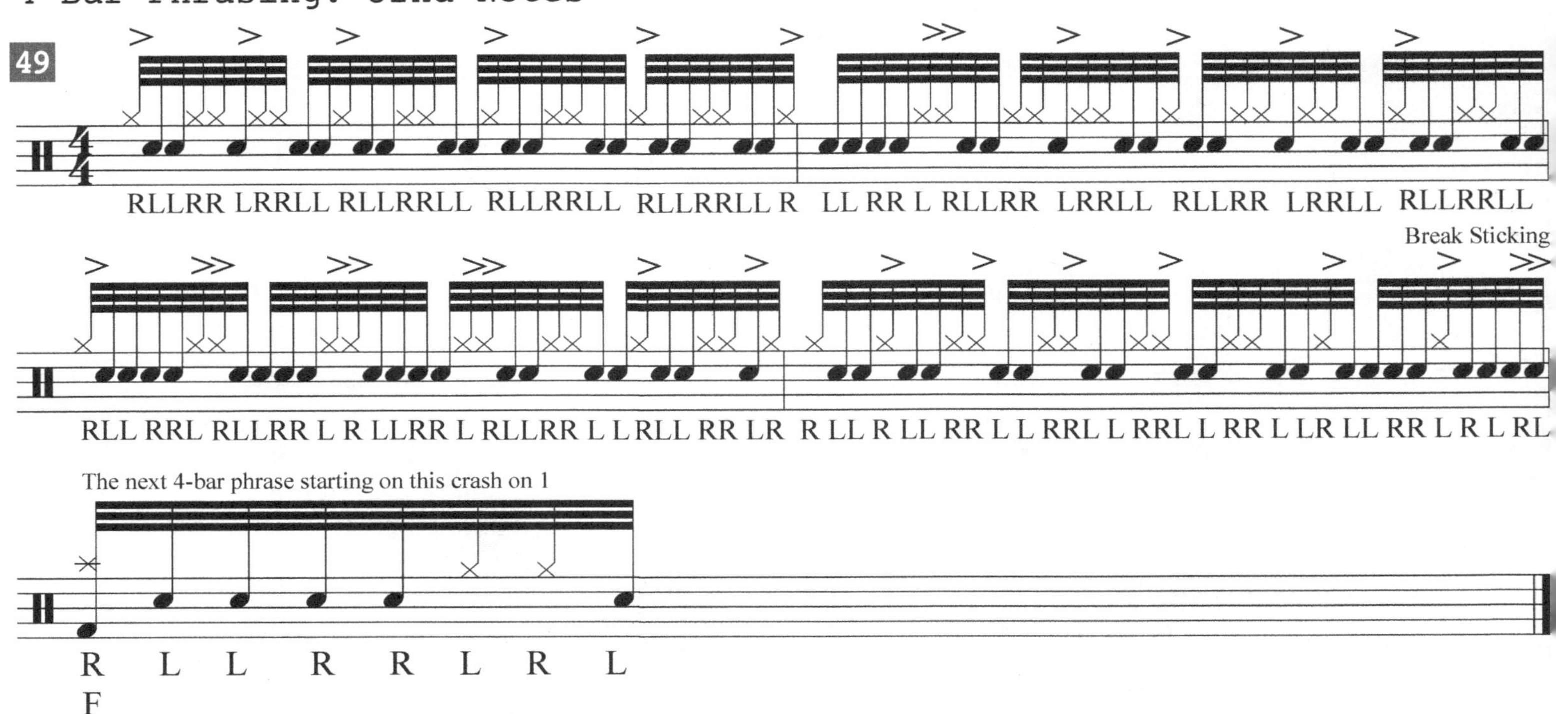

Step IV of Development

Phrase Mixing and Matching

Time to put it all together using the fundamentals: note rate, orchestration, dynamics, and phrasing. A difficult part of this step is to keep outside stickings from creeping into the phrasing. Keeping your focus on only the Glue Stickings from this chapter, limits the amount of stickings to choose from. Limiting the choices, allows you to put more energy into the musical fundamentals you are developing in this chapter. You will decide whether you want to use 4- or 8-bar phrasing.

Glue Stickings Included

-RLLRRL-

-RLLR-

-RLLRRLRRLL-

-RLLRRLL-

Step 4: You will choose one Glue Sticking at a time, performed consecutively, applied to all note rates introduced thus far. You will again use improvisation to choose your Glue Stickings while utilizing a 4-bar phrase format. At the end of the 4th bar, you will crash on the 1, with the idea that you are allowed to break any of the chosen Glue Stickings on the 4th beat of the 4th bar to get to the 1. We are continuing to strengthen the ability to break stickings, while adding a stronger element of musicality. Remember, continuing to loop the 4-bar phrase after you crash on the 1 is important… "DON'T STOP!"; that's what I yell at my students. The left foot keeps 8th note pulse with the hi-hat if you are not utilizing your hi-hat in a closed state. Metronome set at 50bpm.

4-Bar Phrasing: All note rates included with minimal orchestration

The next 4-bar phrase starting on this crash on 1

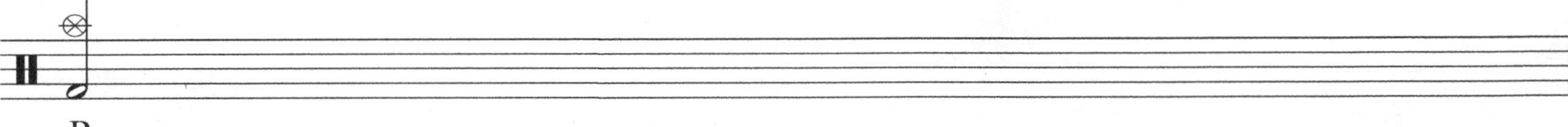

CHAPTER 3

Consecutive Kick Variations

Chapter 3

Glue Sticking Category #3

Consecutive Kick Variations

The stickings in this final category will have two consecutive kick drums in each sticking. Creating a list of stickings with a variety of characteristics is important to diversifying the application to the drum set. Having variation in each separate category of Glue Stickings helps support the use of the "Sectioning Concept" that we will utilize later in the book.

Chapter 3 Stickings Introduced

Consecutive Kick Variations

RLRFF

RLRLRFF

RLLFRLF

RFF

Chapter 3

Step I of Development

Physical Independence

The Glue Stickings in this chapter are the most physically challenging in the book. From both my own personal development and my experience working with students, your balance is challenged at a high level when combining your left foot timekeeping with consecutive right foot movements. While practicing, utilize slower tempos to help develop a healthy level of patience with your body's muscle memory. Remember, this step is not to develop a musical application of the stickings, but to allow your body to create physical confidence in its motion. Your body, when relaxed and confident, will allow you to focus on what you are playing rather than how you are playing. A slower tempo on the metronome will give your limbs a relaxed anticipation of motion.

Consecutive Kick Variations

1st Glue Sticking: *RLRFF*

Step 1: Perform 1st Glue Sticking at each designated note rate. Left foot keeps 8th note pulse with hi-hat. Also, apply these dynamic values one at a time. Metronome set at 50bpm.

Dynamic Values

RLRFF / RLRFF / RLRFF

(accent marks: > over the first R of the first group; >> over the second group; > over the final R of the third group)

Note Rate: 8th-Note Triplets (First Dynamic Shape)

Note Rate: 16th Notes

Note Rate: 16th-Note Triplets

Note Rate: 32nd Notes

Consecutive Kick Variations

2nd Glue Sticking: *RLRLRFF*

Step 1: Perform 2nd Glue Sticking at each designated note rate. Left foot keeps 8th note pulse with hi-hat. Also, apply these dynamic values one at a time. Metronome set at 50bpm.

Dynamic Values

> >> >>

RLRLRFF / RLRLRFF / RLRLRFF

Note Rate: 8th-Note Triplets (First Dynamic Shape)

55

Note Rate: 16th Notes

56

Note Rate: 16th-Note Triplets

57

Note Rate: 32nd Notes

58

3rd Glue Sticking: RLLFFRLF

Step 1: Perform 3rd Glue Sticking at each designated note rate. Left foot keeps 8th note pulse with hi-hat. Also, apply these dynamic values one at a time. Metronome set at 50bpm.

Dynamic Values

RLLFFRLF / RLLFFRLF

Note Rate: 8th-Note Triplets (First Dynamic Shape)

59

Note Rate: 16th Notes

60

Note Rate: 16th-Note Triplets

61

Note Rate: 32nd Notes

62

Consecutive Kick Variations

4th Glue Sticking: *RFF*

Step 1: Perform 4th Glue Sticking at each designated note rate. Left foot keeps 8th note pulse with hi-hat. Also, apply these dynamic values one at a time. Metronome set at 50bpm.

Dynamic Values

>
RFF / RFF

Note Rate: 8th-Note Triplets (First Dynamic Shape)

Note Rate: 16th Notes

Note Rate: 16th-Note Triplets

Note Rate: 32nd Notes

Chapter 3

Step II of Development

Audible Independence

These Glue Stickings are hard! Remember to keep the tempo slow; even if you have developed some speed with Step 1, and are feeling confident, exercise that confidence with patience. You will be using a cycle, orchestration, and dynamic value for each of these consecutive kick Glue Stickings. The slower tempo will help to open your ears to the musical characteristics of the Glue Stickings as well as the meter and time. Honor the choices that I have made for the application of the Glue Stickings to the kit and follow the natural flow of the cycle. Remember to be patient with your ears as you develop the ability to hear both the cycle and the environment simultaneously. The environment is defined by the metronome and meter.

Creating Cycles

Step 2: Perform each of the "Consecutive Kick Variation" stickings in four voice orchestration (kick, snare, mid tom, floor tom) in the order you find below. You will play through each sticking two times without stopping in between each sticking. This creates the cycle. Also, you will be using a new set of dynamic values to create a contrasting musical shape. Metronome set at 50bpm.

Dynamic Values

RLRFF / RLRLRFF / RLLFFRLF / RFF

Cycle Applied to 8th-Note Triplets

Cycle Applied to 16th Notes

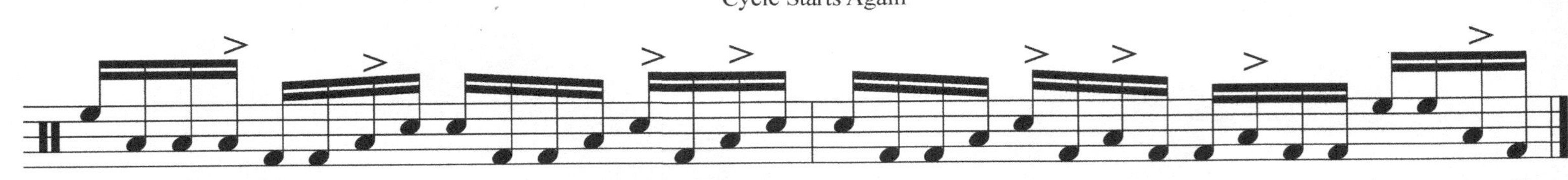

Cycle Applied to 16th-Note Triplets

Cycle Applied to 32nd Notes

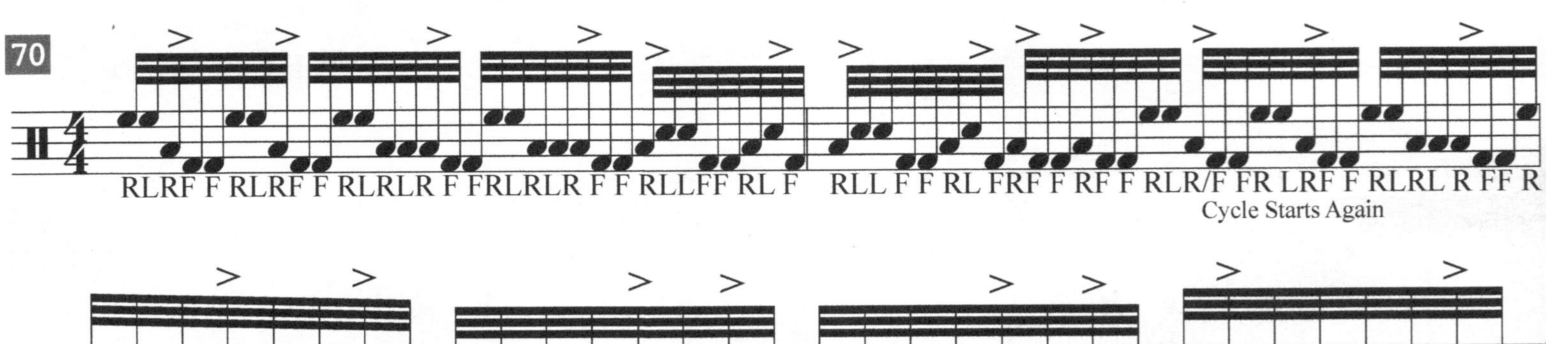

Chapter 3

Step III of Development

Phrase Breaking

Time to make some choices! Use the Glue Stickings from this chapter to improvise your way to the 1. Once you select which Glue Sticking to play, make sure you complete the Glue Sticking in its entirety, as we are developing the ability to anticipate the choice when we need to get to the 1. The choice to break the Glue Sticking you are playing will also include your ability to hear what you are creating throughout the phrase. Not only will your choices become more musical as you practice this step, your ability to anticipate a way back to the 1 will get stronger.

Consecutive Kick Variations

Glue Stickings Included

-RLRFF-
-RLRLRFF-
-RLLFFRLF-
-RFF-

Step 3: You will choose one Glue Sticking at a time, performed consecutively, applied to one chosen note rate. Continue to make choices with an improvisational function utilizing a 4-bar phrase format. At the end of the 4th bar, you will crash on the 1, with the idea that you are allowed to break any of the chosen Glue Stickings on the 4th beat of the 4th bar to get to the 1. This strengthened my ability to break my stickings to get to ensemble figures or natural cadences. As for the dynamic and orchestration choices, the only rule I followed was to keep it simple. If you have done your work with step 1 and 2, your body will make choices dynamically and musically from those steps. Left foot will be involved with holding the hi-hat in the down position. Metronome set at 50bpm.

4-Bar Phrasing: 8th-Note Triplets

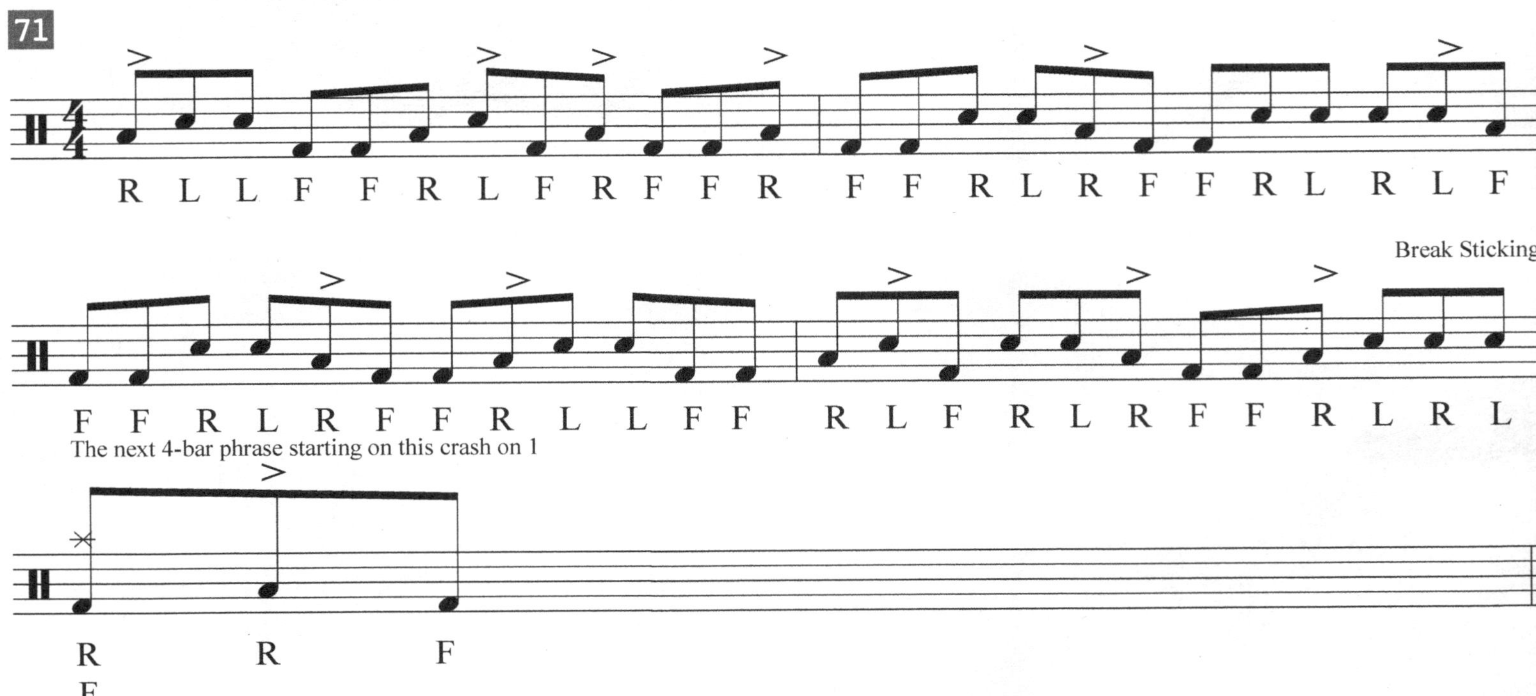

4-Bar Phrasing: 16th Notes

72

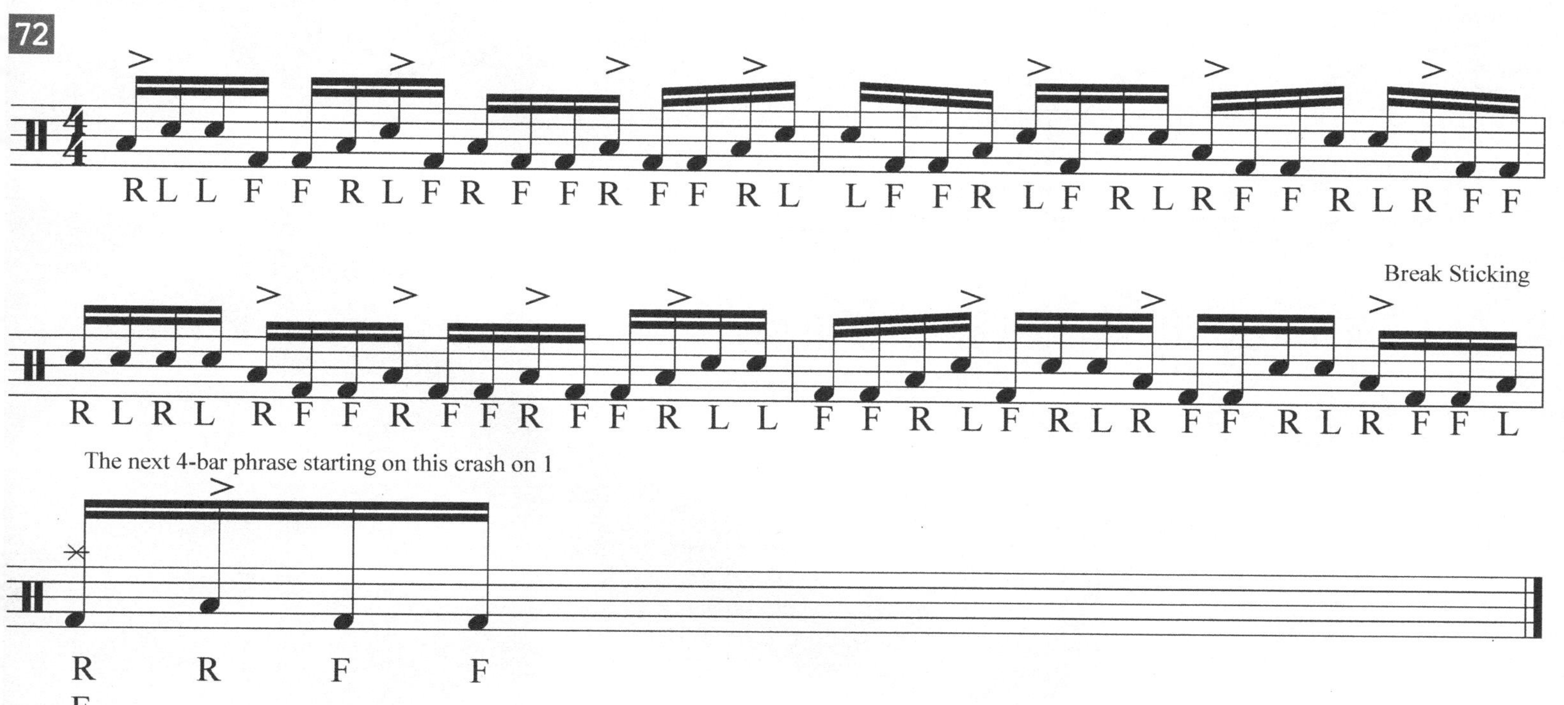

4-Bar Phrasing: 16th-Note Triplets

73

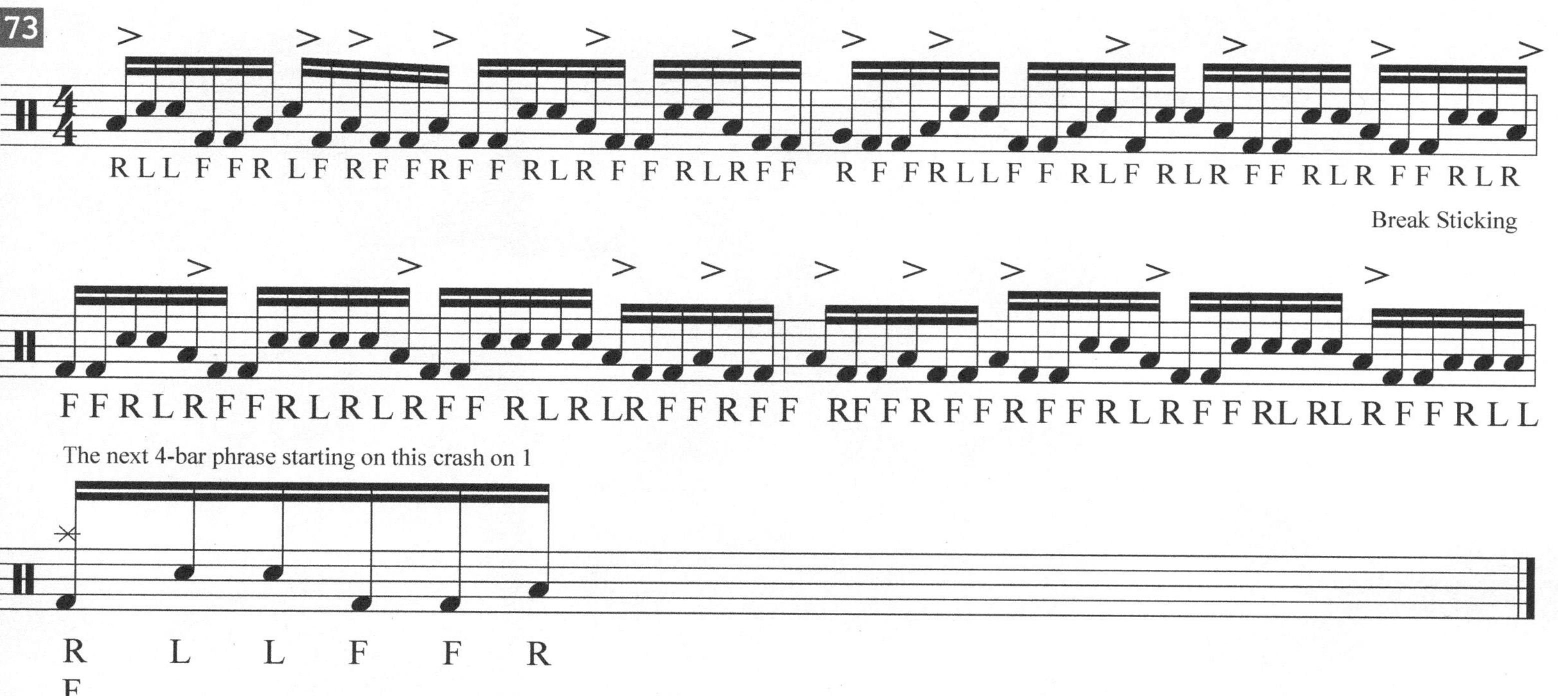

4-Bar Phrasing: 32nd Notes

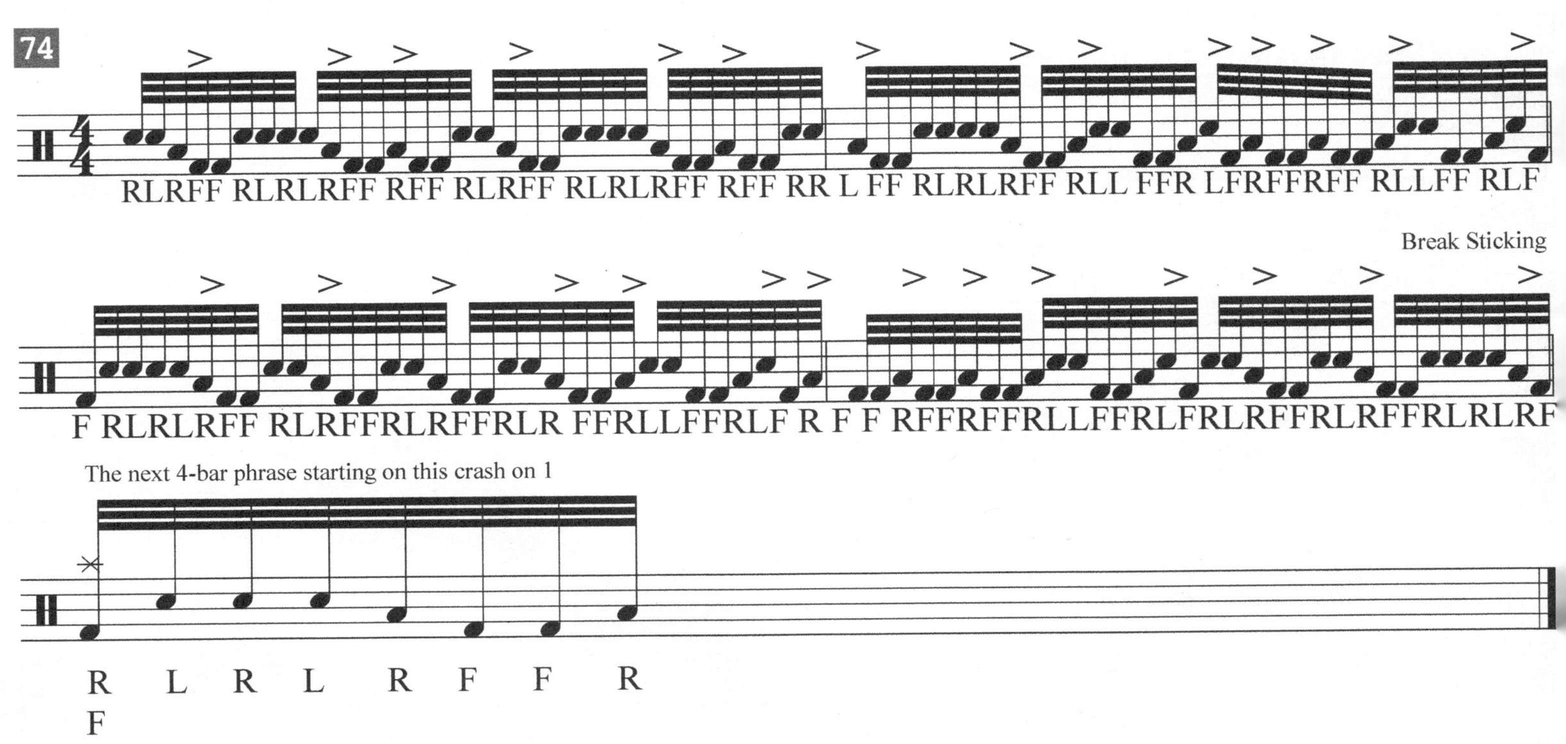

Chapter 3

Step IV of Development

Phrase Mixing and Matching

Stay focused with only the Glue Stickings from this chapter! You will have the urge to use Glue Stickings from previous chapters, but by exercising restraint, you are helping to reinforce the power of choice and focus. While mixing and matching, you are building upon the foundation that you have developed with the first three steps:

Step 1: Physical Independence, so your body feels free.

Step 2: Audible Independence, so your ears are open.

Step 3: Phrase Breaking, so you can get to where you need to go.

Trust the foundation and start to build musicality now!

Consecutive Kick Variations

Glue Stickings Included

-RLRFF-

-RLRLRFF-

-RLRFFRLF-

-RFF-

Step 4: You will choose one Glue Sticking at a time, performed consecutively, applied to all note rates introduced thus far. You will again use improvisation to choose your Glue Stickings while utilizing a 4-bar phrase format. At the end of the 4th bar, you will crash on the 1, with the idea that you are allowed to break any of the chosen Glue Stickings on the 4th beat of the 4th bar to get to the 1. We are continuing to strengthen the ability to break stickings, while adding a stronger element of musicality. Remember, continuing to loop the 4-bar phrase after you crash on the 1 is important… "DON'T STOP!"; that's what I yell at my students. Left foot keeps 8th note pulse with the hi-hat if you are not utilizing your hi-hat in a closed state. Metronome set at 50bpm.

4-Bar Phrasing: All note rates included with minimal orchestration

CHAPTER 4

The Master Cycle

Chapter 4

"The Master Cycle"

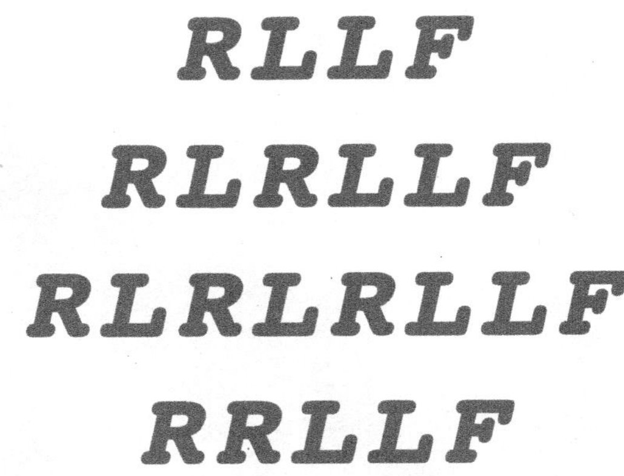

RLLF

RLRLLF

RLRLRLLF

RRLLF

RLLRRL

RLLR

RLLRRLRRLL

RLLRRLL

RLRFF

RLRLRFF

RLLFFRLF

RFF

Chapter 4

The Master Cycle: a *must* for your daily practice

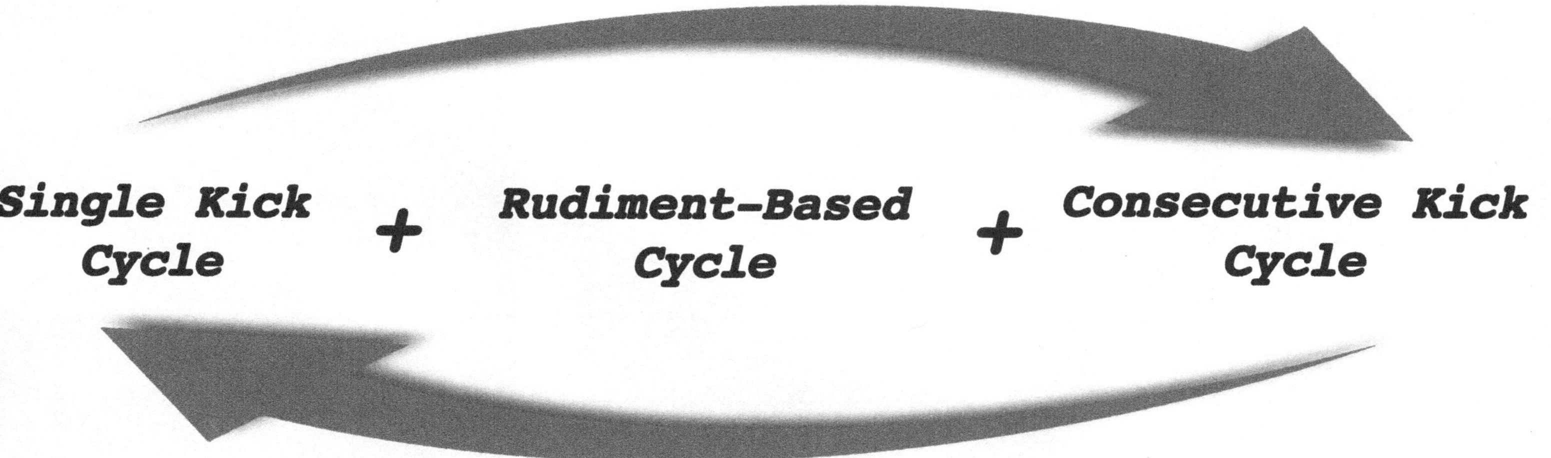

The Master Cycle is the combination of each individual cycle, developed in Chapters 1, 2 and 3, linked together to create a longer, more complex routine-based exercise for daily practice. Incorporating the Master Cycle into daily practice is the key to consistent development of the Glue Method. This routine encompasses musicality, independence, dynamics and orchestration.

To run the Master Cycle, pick a note rate and tempo; then, start with the Single Kick Variation Cycle, then move to the Rudiment-Based Cycle, then end with the Consecutive Kick Variations, before looping back to the Single Kick Variations. Before you begin, note that there is one musical change to the orchestration in the Single Kick Variation Cycle. We will be substituting your left foot for your right foot. Your left foot will chick the hi-hat in each of the stickings, instead of the right foot striking the bass drum. This change will help to create the feeling of flowing across the kit from left to right, ending the Master Cycle with the low tones on the kit. To challenge yourself, pick different note rates and tempos and continue to run all of the Glue Stickings. Throughout the exercise, remember to honor the orchestration and dynamics from the individual cycles.

The Master Cycle was invaluable to me because it was made up of the same stickings that I was using in my soloing. The Master Cycle was a simple and effective way to create a practical exercise in my practice routine. This exercise gave me the confidence that I could continue to listen to the metronome and the meter, while honoring the Glue Stickings, orchestrations, and dynamic values from step 2 of each of the categories of Glue Stickings. Eventually this exercise replaced an individual development of each category.

Master Cycle applied to 8th-Note Triplets

Master Cycle applied to 16th Notes

Master Cycle applied to 16th-Note Triplets

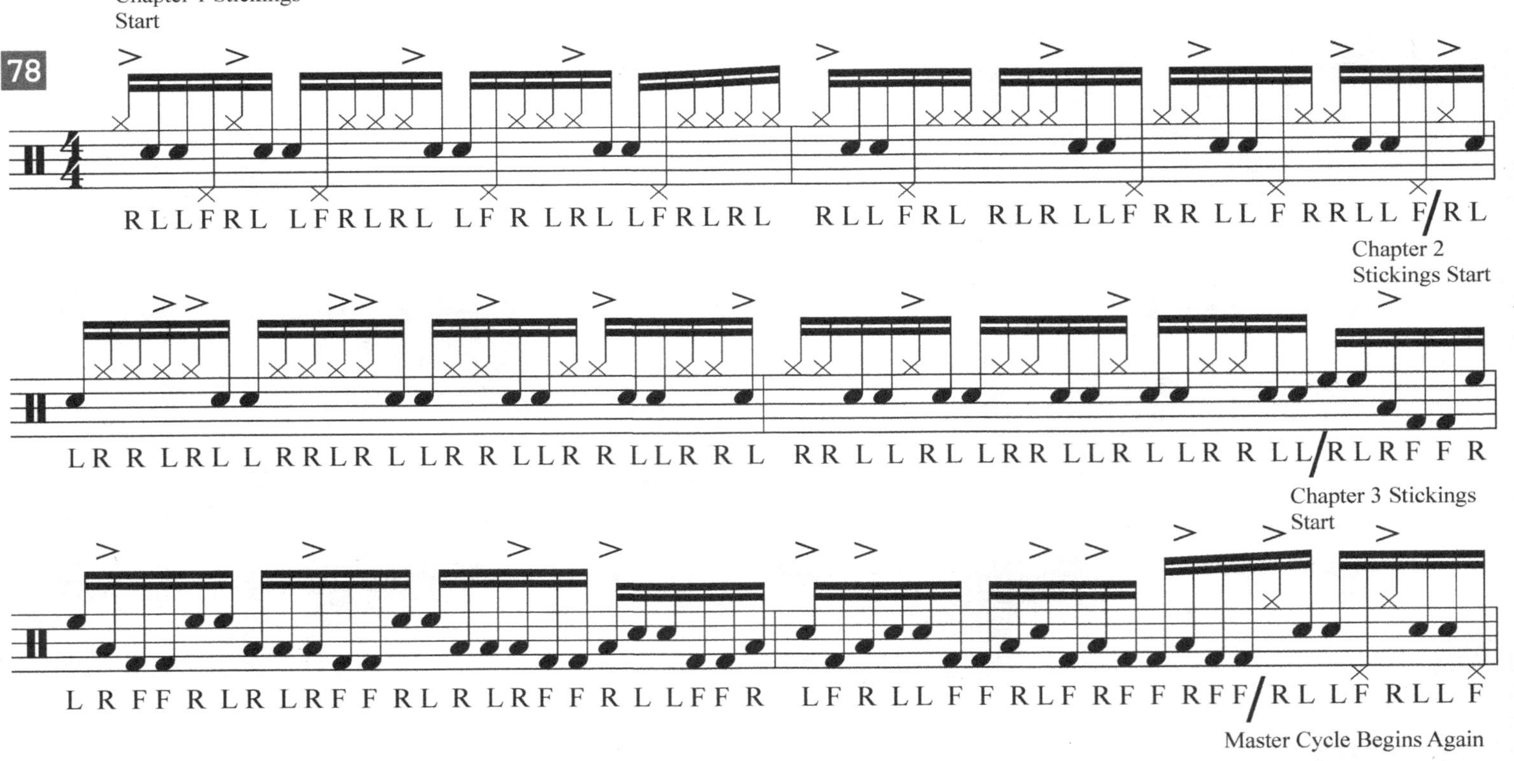

Master Cycle applied to 32nd Notes

CHAPTER 5
Sectioning Concept

Chapter 5

Sectioning: An Organizational Concept for Glue Stickings

Single Kick / Rudiment-Based / Consecutive Kick

Sectioning is an organizational concept that assigns each Glue Sticking category to a specific section of the drum set. By creating these sections, more of my consciousness was available to be in the moment, stay calm and stay one step ahead compositionally. This final step of the Glue Method will help you to stay calm and clear with your choices as well. Note rates, dynamics, orchestration and phrasing are the fundamentals that you will utilize to make your Glue Sticking choices musical. Listening to how your Glue Sticking choices respond to each other in a more compositional environment is crucial to making a solo musical. Having these parameters in the practice room will give you more freedom to be in the moment when performing, and not in your head trying to think of what to play next.

To apply the concept of sectioning, you will be playing 4 bars of each Glue Sticking category improvisationally applied to the corresponding section of the drum set. At the end of each 4-bar phrase, you will be crashing on 1 of the next 4-bar phrase.

Listen to yourself and your choices, record yourself and listen back, be reflective, make changes and learn from them!

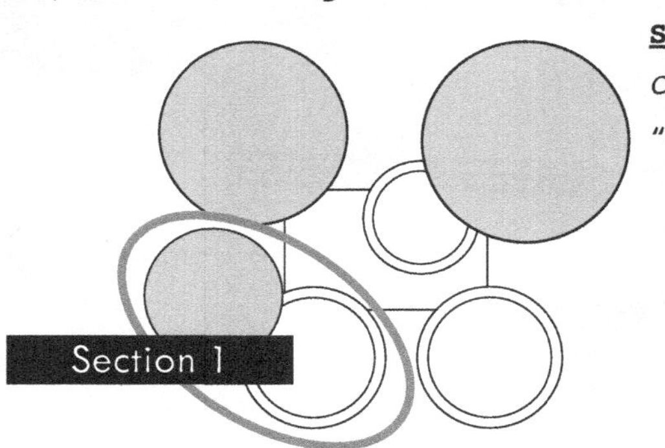

SECTION 1

Category #1

"Single Kick Variations"

SECTION 3

Category #3

"Consecutive Kick Variations"

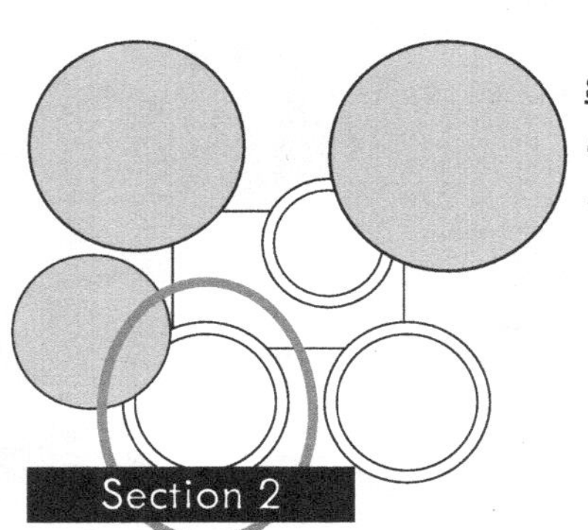

SECTION 2

Category #2

"Rudiment-Based Variations"

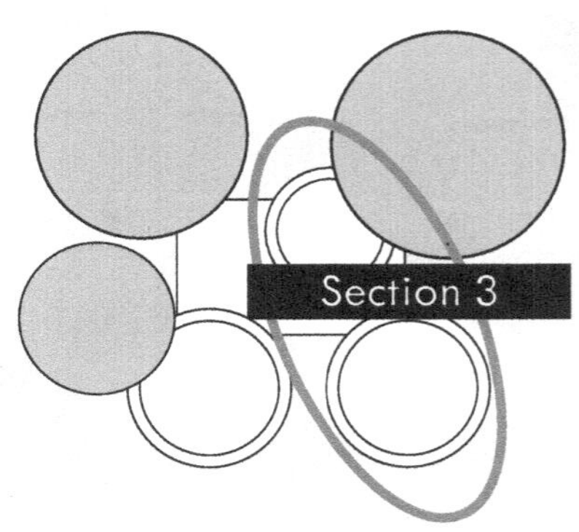

8-Bar Phrasing: All note rates and Glue Stickings

SECTION 1

80

R L R L L F R L L F R R L L F R R L L F R L R L L F R L L F R L L F R R L L F R

Break Sticking

R L L F R L R L L F R R L L F R L R L R L L F R L R L R L L F R R L R L

The next 4-bar phrase starting on this crash on 1

RLRLR R L L F R RL L F R R L L F R R L L F R L L F R L L F R L R L L F R L R L
F

Break Sticking

R L L F R L L F R R L L F R R L L F R L L F R R L L F R L R L R L L F R R L R L R L

The next 4-bar phrase starting on this crash on 1

SECTION 2

R L L R R L R L L R R L R R L L R L L R R L R R L L R L L R R L R
F

Break Sticking

R L L R L L R R L R L L R R L L R R L L R R L R R L L R L L R R L L R R L L R

The next 4-bar phrase starting on this crash on 1

L R R L L R L L R R L R L L R R L R L L R R L R L L R R L L R R L L R L L R R

Break Sticking

L L R L L R R L R R L L R L L R R L R L L R R L R L L R R L L R L R R L

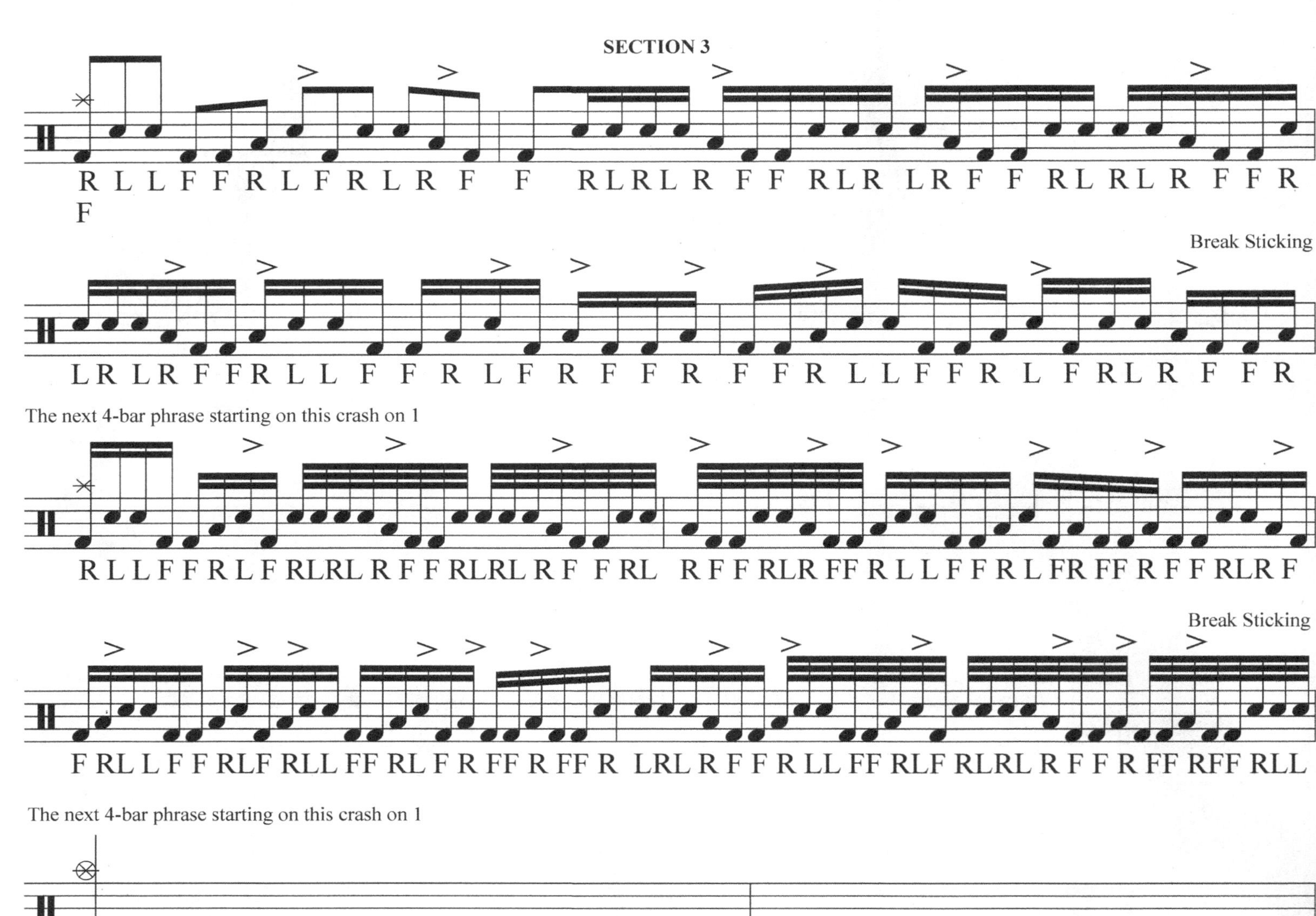
SECTION 3
R L L F F R L F R L R F F RLRL R F F RLR LR F F RL RL R F F R
F
Break Sticking
LR LR F FR L L F F R L F R F F R F F R L L F F R L F RL R F F R
The next 4-bar phrase starting on this crash on 1
R L L F F R L F RLRL R F F RLRL R F F RL R F F RLR FF R L L F F R L FR FF R F F RLR F
Break Sticking
F RL L F F RLF RLL FF RL F R FF R FF R LRL R F F R LL FF RLF RLRL R F F R FF RFF RLL
The next 4-bar phrase starting on this crash on 1

Conclusion

Goals and Expectations for Each Step of Development

The foundation that you have begun to develop while working through the Glue Method, is made up of fundamentals that I have identified over my career as a performer and as an educator. In the Star Diagram, the word "You" is at the top. "You" will bring these stickings to life... "You" will create the music as you continue to work through the steps of development. "You" represents your sound, interpretation, and touch. Help support your journey by taking your time with the steps of development and with the application of your interpretation of the Glue Stickings. Don't rush to introduce every note rate with every Glue Sticking in every orchestration in the first fifteen seconds of your solo. Consider what you are trying to create, consider what the band is playing, and try not to rush the listener. Don't forget, repetition is a powerful tool and what you might think sounds boring or slow, someone else might find exciting and beautiful. Good luck and have FUN! Here are some thoughts on each step; keep them in mind.

I
Physical Independence

Allow your body to soak up this step; don't rush past this development. Physical independence has no shortcuts! Give your body time to develop the appropriate amount of independence, as this will allow the subsequent steps to follow smoothly, because of the foundation this step creates.

II
Audible Independence

The development of your ability to listen can be frustrating. This skill, as it is being developed, is not always front and center, but trust me, it is happening. The first glimpse will be your ability to hear where the metronome is putting the 1 while you phrase. Next, you will start to be aware of the bigger picture of what you are creating and even the ability to check in with what the band is playing.

III
Phrase Breaking

Anticipating your way out of the improvisation is crucial to the success of your FLOW! Stick to the simplicity in this step. When you break the stickings, don't try to make the choices too complicated. Being more creative during those moments of breaking the Glue Stickings takes time.

IV
Phrase Mixing and Matching

Again, keep your choices simple and remember that repetition is powerful. Listeners love to recognize phrases and this can help create an interaction with the listener. Pay attention to your accuracy, clarity, dynamics, and consistency. Don't lose control of what you are creating; the previous steps will empower you to stay focused.

Thank You

It has always been a dream of mine to write an instructional book. The Glue Method was created as part of my individual journey to overcome obstacles that were preventing me from achieving my goals on the drum set. Honoring my passion for teaching and following my dream, I wrote this book to help my fellow drummers, as it can now be just as powerful of a tool for them as it was for me.

Thank you to Rob Wallis and Joe Bergamini at Hudson Music for giving me this opportunity and believing in the project.

Thank you to Terry Branam for your diligence, creativity and support.

Thank you to my mentor, colleague and dear friend Dave DiCenso for the constant support and guidance, not only on the drum set, but in life as well.

Thank you to Vater Percussion, Remo Drum Heads, Zildjian Cymbals, and Pearl Drums for your consistent and continued support.

And, to my family, your love fuels my fire. Thank you to my wife Ashley for always pushing and supporting my dreams without question or hesitation. And, thank you to my children, Eli and Emma, for always inspiring me to work my hardest everyday.

Notes

Notes